The Ultimate Disney Vacation Club Guide

The Ultimate Disney Vacation Club Guide

Shaun Brouwer

Theme Park Press
www.ThemeParkPress.com

Theme Park Press publishes its books in a variety of print and electronic formats. Some content that appears in one format may not appear in another.

Editor: Bob McLain
Layout: Artisanal Text

ISBN 978-1-941500-78-1
Printed in the United States of America

Theme Park Press | www.ThemeParkPress.com
Address queries to bob@themeparkpress.com

To my wonderfully supportive wife, Jamie; you have always supported my love for Disney and encouraged me to follow my dreams. I love you!

Contents

Introduction

I became a Disney fanatic at an early age. I grew up on Disney, visiting Disney World every year during spring break with my family, reading books about the theme parks, listening to Disney music, and watching Disney movies. My first memory of Walt Disney World dates back to 1984. Up until that point, my family had stopped at Disney World for the day during trips to Florida, but we had never actually stayed on Disney property. The previous year, 1983, marked my father's 10-year anniversary with his employer, and as a reward for being a loyal employee for all those years, the company offered to pay for our next family vacation. Now, my dad was never one to splurge, but since the company was paying for it, he decided that this time he would do just that. And so began our first Disney trip the following spring.

Walt Disney World was much different then. There were only two theme parks—the Magic Kingdom and the recently opened Epcot Center—and only a handful of Disney hotels. We didn't technically stay at a Disney resort; we stayed at the Viscount Hotel, across the street from the Disney Village Marketplace (more recently known as Downtown Disney and currently Disney Springs), so we were basically on Disney property.

This was my first memory of WDW, and boy did it make an impression on me! We did a lot of great things on that trip, incluidng a character breakfast with Chip 'n' Dale on the Empress Lilly, dinner at the Polynesian Luau, and visits to the parks, of course. The trip got our family hooked on Disney World. My parents wanted to come back each year, but needed to figure out a way to do that without breaking the bank, and Disney had a solution: Fort Wilderness Campground. We had always been campers, and had a pop-up camper that we used for shorter trips during the summer—mostly in local campgrounds and state parks. Since we already had a camper, staying at Fort Wilderness was a natural choice; we just had to tow the camper a little farther—over a thousand miles this time!

And so began our yearly spring break treks to Walt Disney World. Our trips weren't extravagant, but as kids we thought they were great. The theming of Fort Wilderness was perfect for me and my two older brothers. On top of that, the Contemporary Resort was just a boat ride away, and had what any kid growing up in the 1980s would love—a gigantic arcade known as the Fiesta Fun Center. And once we were at the Contemporary, getting anywhere else was easy, thanks to the monorail.

We usually only went to one park each year, but since there were only two parks at that time it didn't really seem like a big deal to us. There was a seemingly endless amount of activities at Fort Wilderness, and Disney World as a whole, to keep us plenty busy. We would visit the now-closed River Country water park, Discovery Island zoological park in the middle of Bay Lake, and rent bikes or canoes for the day. As time went on and my older brothers moved out and started their own families and it got to be just me and my parents on Disney trips, my dad started to get a little tired of lugging that pop-up camper all the way down to Florida each year, so we started staying at Value resorts during our visits to the park.

When I met my wife I was thrilled to find out that she, too, grew up visiting Disney World each year. For our honeymoon, I don't think either of us gave it a second thought: we were going to Disney World. We had a magical honeymoon at Wilderness Lodge, with a Disney cruise tacked on. We assumed we'd vacation at Disney World each year, just as we'd done when we were kids, but reality (and kids of our own) set in. Our visits became less frequent.

On one of those visits, we noticed that Disney was going to be giving a presentation on the Disney Vacation Club (DVC) My wife wanted to go and listen to it, but I was hesitant. We had a bad time-share presentation experience once, and I didn't want to go through that again. Plus, wasn't the Disney Vacation Club for rich people? Despite these reservations, we decided to attend.

We were pleasantly surprised to find that it was a very informative and low-pressure presentation, and both of us really liked what we heard. I started running the numbers in my head and began to realize that joining the DVC might be just the thing to enable us to resume our yearly visits to Disney World. The hardest part would be coming up with the money to buy in, but I figured I could sell my travel trailer and use that money to buy into the club. And while there are recurring yearly costs for owning a DVC contract (maintenance fees), I reasoned that I would still be ahead because these fees would be much less than what I was paying for insurance, storage, and maintenance on my travel trailer. There were also financing options for buying in, but I really didn't want to go down that route if I didn't have to. The biggest revelation to me in all of this was that we could lock in our yearly vacations at today's prices for the next 40–50 years!

As great as it all sounded, there was something holding us back. I wanted to do more research. I'm not one to make big financial decisions on a whim. So we gathered as much information as we could from that presentation, packed it in our suitcases, and took it home with us. The real work was soon to come.

Once we returned home, I started on a massive quest to research DVC as thoroughly as I possibly could and make sure it was the right thing for our family. What I found through my research amazed me. There was a way to buy into DVC at a fraction of the cost that I was quoted in the presentation, something that many folks overlook or just simply aren't aware of: resale DVC contracts.

My original intention for this book was to take a detailed look at the process of buying a resale DVC contract. Instead, I decided to take a more holistic approach, first looking at how to determine if DVC is right for you, then how to buy into DVC, and finally how to best use your DVC contract. Along the way I will detail everything you need to know to make informed decisions.

It is not my intention with this book to convince you to buy into the Disney Vacation Club. I'm sure my enthusiasm for DVC will show through, but I realize that it's not for everybody. The worst thing that you can do is buy into DVC when it is really not the best fit for you.

But if it *is* a great fit, I want to help you realize that dream.

ONE

What Is the Disney Vacation Club?

Throughout this book I will give you a detailed look at all the different aspects of the Disney Vacation Club, buying and using DVC, discounts, tricks, and more. But before looking at the finer details of buying and using the Disney Vacation Club, let me first introduce you to it. This chapter is the short "Cliff's Notes" explanation of DVC. Let's dive in!

Disney has often called the DVC program the "best-kept secret" of Disney vacationing, and that must be true because I'm amazed at times when I tell people I'm a member of the Disney Vacation Club and find out they have no idea of what that means—usually they think it's a discount club. Simply put, DVC is a pre-paid vacation—a timeshare. The word "timeshare" often raises red flags and is enough to scare people off. Many of us have sat through long timeshare presentations after we've been told we've won a "free" vacation or received a "free" gift.

The first experience I had attending a timeshare presentation was horrible. My wife and I were approaching our first anniversary and one day she received a call offering a free weekend stay at one of our favorite hotels, along with a free dinner at an upscale restaurant. This sounded terrific to her,; some might even say it sounded "too good to be true". My wife decided she would surprise me by booking this "free" vacation. The only stipulation was attending a "short" sales tour of their timeshare property, and my wife was assured we were under no obligation to buy. She sprung the trip on me and it sounded great to me, too; how bad could the sales tour be, right?

We were both so very wrong, as we were about to find out.

While the hotel stay was great, the sales tour was horrible, and one of the worst experiences of our lives. The tour itself was long, but fairly uneventful. After we were taken around the property to see the various amenities, each couple was seated at a round table in a large room so that we could talk with a sales associate. These highly energetic people told us about their deals, which of course were only good if we signed up on the spot that day. I told the first sales associate that, while their property was beautiful, we didn't have the money to purchase into their timeshare. Immediately, they started in with financing options. I countered that I don't like to make big financial decisions like this on the spot and prefer to have time to weigh all options and make a more educated and informed decision. Finally, the sales associate relented and told us we would have to meet with his supervisor before we could leave.

When his supervisor came over, she went through the exact same spiel to try to get us to buy in, and we gave the exact same arguments as to why we wouldn't be buying it. Finally, she also relented, but informed us that we would have to meet with the sales manager before we could leave. She brought over her sales manager, and this guy was a piece of work. He would not take no for an answer. We felt trapped by this point, and my blood was starting to boil. He asked me why we didn't want to buy their timeshare and I repeated that my wife and I don't like to make big decisions without taking time to weigh all options and make an informed decision. At this point, the sales manager turns to my wife with a wry smirk on his face and says "Boy, it sounds like if you're at the grocery store and want to buy something, you have to call your husband first to see if it's ok".

I'm usually fairly mild mannered, but that made me lose it. I stood up and screamed at the guy that he had no right to speak to us like this and let him know that he personally insulted me. Keep in mind, there was a room full of other families meeting with sales people wanting to buy in, so the sales manager was begging me to stop screaming. His sales associate was in tears, as was my wife. We left there and I felt terrible that I had lost my temper and made my wife cry (I didn't care too much about the sales associate being in tears), so I apologized to my wife for losing control.

Needless to say, this experience soured both of us on the prospect of ever purchasing a timeshare.

Fast forward ten years. Although I was a huge Disney World fan I was wary of the Disney Vacation Club because I already knew that it was a timeshare. When I finally took a good, hard look at DVC, I was pleased to find that, while it is similar to a timeshare in that you are buying a real-estate interest in a Disney resort, it is different in that it offers so much more flexibility, and the sales associates are not high pressure as was the case with our previous timeshare experience. Unlike a traditional, fixed-week timeshare, the Disney Vacation Club is a points-based system. The number of vacation points you buy is based on your vacationing habits—which resorts you typically stay at, what type of room, time of the year, etc. Once you buy into the program, you receive vacation points each year that you can use however you would like. You can stay for one night, two nights, a week, or however long you want as long as you have enough points. The Disney Vacation Club offers such flexibility to accommodate all types of vacationers. You can stay at any time of year as long as there is availability at the time you book your vacation. Most would assume that joining DVC locks you into vacationing only at a Disney resort, but that's not the case—there are literally thousands of other resorts around the world where you can use your vacation points. The two key aspects of the Disney Vacation Club that sold me on it were its flexibility and the financial benefits and perks of being a DVC member.

So, at this point you may be asking: "What's so great about paying a large sum of money now so that you can vacation in the future?"

It's simple: you are essentially locking in today's prices for the next 50 years. The number of points required to reserve a room does not increase over time like the cost of a hotel room typically would increase year after year. In fact, in many cases buying a DVC contract will pay for itself in the first 5–10 years that you own it, and sometimes even less when you take into account all of the discounts you are eligible for as a DVC member. It is important to note that there *are* recurring costs involved with a DVC purchase. Each year you will have to pay maintenance fees on your contract. The amount of these fees varies based on your home resort and the number of points that you own. We will get into the financial details of a DVC purchase in subsequent chapters of this book.

As a DVC member, you will receive many perks and discounts that other Disney guests don't receive. Some of these perks include shopping and dining discounts, access to special events, and discounts on annual passes. You also have more room choices—DVC has everything from deluxe studios that sleep 4–5 guests, all the way up to three-bedroom grand villas that sleep 9–12 guests. All DVC rooms have some sort of kitchen, whether a small kitchenette with a microwave, sink, and mini fridge in the studios, or a full kitchen in the one-bedroom and larger rooms.

You may wonder why a kitchen in your room is a perk—you're on vacation, right? Why would you want a kitchen? It is a great way to save money at Disney. The food at WDW is great, but taking a family out to eat for three meals a day isn't cheap, especially at the table-service restaurants. Having a kitchen allows you to save both time and money, even if you use it for just one meal per day. For example, if you want to get to the parks early in the morning to beat the crowds, whip up a quick breakfast in your room and you're on your way.

Another great feature of DVC is that Disney gives you the option of using up to 3 years of points in one shot by "banking" and "borrowing" points, allowing for a truly magical vacation experience. There are many ways to maximize your vacation points using the banking and borrowing features—this is a subject we will explore in much more detail later on in this book. Again, the key idea behind DVC is flexibility—Disney wants their vacation club members to have as many options as possible because not everyone vacations the same way.

The DVC presence at Walt Disney World has grown exponentially since its introduction in 1992, and it shows no signs of slowing down. DVC started with one resort in WDW in 1992 and there are now nearly a dozen DVC resorts on property. Disney has also expanded to locations in Hawaii (Disney's Aulani Resort), California (Disney's Grand Californian Resort at Disneyland), South Carolina (Disney Hilton Head Island Resort), and Florida's Atlantic Coast (Disney's Vero Beach Resort). While DVC resorts offer a lot for members, it is also a huge financial benefit to the Disney Company. More members means more people in the parks, more people buying souvenirs, and more people buying food. More members means more people visiting the resort year after year.

In fact, the demand for DVC has grown so much recently that Disney has a tough time keeping up. If you look at resort expansions over the past 10 years at Walt Disney World, most of it has been building new DVC resorts or adding a DVC component to existing resorts, as was recently done at both the Grand Floridian and Polynesian Village. Disney has a hard time filling deluxe hotel rooms, especially during slow times of the year. There just aren't enough people who can afford deluxe resorts, and many that can afford it still opt for the moderate or even value resorts. But, as any DVC member who has tried to get a reservation at a DVC resort less than 7 months before their trip knows, DVC resorts book up fast!

The amount of points required to stay at a DVC resort varies widely by the resort, type of room, and season of the year. DVC resorts typically have five different seasons, ranging from the Adventure Season that includes the least busiest times of the year (January and September) to the Premier Season which includes the busiest times (spring break and Christmas/New Year's). One of the great things about being a DVC member is that when you are booking a DVC resort, you don't have to put down a monetary deposit, because you've already paid for it up front when you purchased your contract.

As mentioned earlier, DVC members are not locked into staying exclusively at a Disney resort. These destinations are broken into three categories: the Disney Collection, the Concierge Collection, and the World Collection. The Disney Collection includes all non-DVC Disney destinations such as non-DVC Walt Disney World and Disneyland hotels and the Disney Cruise Line. The Concierge Collection is a group of popular vacation destinations around the world that have been hand-picked by Disney. It includes European destinations, mountain and ski resorts, beach resorts, and cosmopolitan city destinations. The World Collection has by far the most destinations available. It is available through point exchanges with both RCI and the Buena Vista Trading Company. RCI is the largest vacation exchange program in the world, offering weekly and nightly point exchanges at just about any vacation experience you could possibly imagine. The Buena Vista Trading Company offers a portfolio that includes Club Cordial with destinations in Austria and Italy, as well as Club Intrawest with ski, beach, and golf destinations in Canada, Mexico, and the United States.

One aspect of the Disney Vacation Club that differs from typical hotel stays is the way that housekeeping services work. When you stay at a DVC resort, your stay is meant to feel like you are at your home away from home. As such, you won't receive daily housekeeping services, because Disney wants you to have as much privacy as possible. For stays of seven or fewer nights, Disney will provide what is called Trash and Towel Services, typically on day four of your stay. The Trash and Towel service includes emptying the trash and installing new garbage can liners, providing fresh bathroom towels, replacing shampoo facial soap and bath soap, replenishing facial tissues, paper towels, toilet paper, coffee (including sugar and cream), dishwashing liquid, dishwasher detergent, sponges, and laundry detergent. If you are staying eight or more nights at a DVC resort, a full cleaning service will be provided on day four and Trash and Towel service will be provided on day eight, with the cycle repeating again on day twelve. The Full Cleaning Service includes everything listed above for the Trash and Towel Service, plus changing bed linens, vacuuming and dusting, cleaning the bathrooms, cleaning the kitchen, and washing the dishes. Some people may still like to have daily housekeeping, so Disney does offer this option for an added cost. However, if you opt for it you must provide Disney with at least 24-hours' notice.

When I first joined DVC, I did not fully understand that housekeeping would work differently. Upon our first DVC stay, I was somewhat disappointed to learn about it, mainly because I'm just so used to having housekeeping when I stay at a hotel. However, I found that the DVC system worked out nicely. It gives you more of a sense that you are at home. Our family didn't miss the daily housekeeping. In fact, when I think about it, there were many occasions during our "pre-DVC" Disney vacations where we would need to get in the room to change for swimming only to find that we couldn't get in, because it was being cleaned. So, my advice to you is to keep an open mind—maybe you really don't need that daily housekeeping service after all.

DVC contracts are flexible in many other ways, too. There may be times when you are unable to use your yearly allotment of points. While you could bank them as we discussed earlier in this chapter, another option is to rent your points out. Disney allows you to rent out your DVC points just like you would with a real estate interest such as your house. You can do this on your own or use a service to connect you with renters. Another alternative to banking or renting points is transferring points. DVC members have the ability to transfer their points to someone else as a gift. Speaking of gifts, another great feature of DVC is that you can will it to your children. So, even if you buy a DVC contract later in life, you can be confident that your children will be able to use it to make new memories with your grandchildren—what a great legacy to leave! With all of these options, there are some details and fine print that you need to be aware of, and we will dive deeper into each of these subjects.

This chapter has given you a high-level glimpse into the Disney Vacation Club and an overview of how it works. In the rest of this book, we'll look at the intricacies of the program. Prior to joining DVC, you'll want to make sure that the program is a good fit for you. Buying into DVC is not cheap, so you need to fully understand the program and how it will benefit you. As flexible as DVC is, the truth is that it's not a great fit for everybody, so we'll look at reasons why you should or shouldn't buy in.

After that, we'll look at the various methods for buying in. Most assume that you have to buy into DVC directly through Disney, but there is another way that could save you thousands of dollars. We'll look at the pros and cons of each buy-in method. Then we'll look at actually using your DVC membership. We'll look at the discounts and perks that you will be eligible for, some that many existing DVC members aren't even aware of. We'll also look at strategies and tips and tricks for making reservations—especially those hard-to-get ones.

There are many DVC resorts to choose from—most at Walt Disney World as well as a few others outside of WDW. We'll take a look at each resort and give an overview of room types, theming, recreation, shopping, and dining. This book also has a FAQ chapter with some of the most common questions asked by potential DVC members.

So pull down your lap bar. It's going to be a fun ride as we look at Disney's best-kept secret: the Disney Vacation Club!

TWO

Is the DVC Right for You?

Buying into the Disney Vacation Club is a huge financial decision and one that you should never rush into or take lightly. It's very easy to attend a DVC presentation and become enamored by how great it sounds. It may sound so incredible that you want to buy in right there on the spot. I'll admit that I was one of those people at first—what the DVC associates presented to my wife and I during the presentation that we attended during a Disney cruise sounded fabulous. I wanted to buy in right away, and my wife was in total agreement. However, we had to temper our enthusiasm and show patience. Buying into DVC will impact you financially for many years to come, so you'll want to make sure you get it right.

If you've ever attended a non-Disney timeshare presentation, you know that most of them are high-pressure situations, like the experience I shared in chapter 1. Presentations like these are usually easy to turn down because they put you in an uncomfortable position. However, you will find that Disney Vacation Club presentations are typically much, much different. In fact, DVC presentations are at the opposite end of the spectrum from traditional timeshare presentations. DVC associates use a low-pressure strategy to sell their product—they explain DVC and pretty much let the product sell itself.

The low-pressure nature of DVC presentations can make you want to join on the spot because the presentation is so good and the DVC associates are so knowledgeable and approachable. Disney really seems to have figured out a great strategy for selling DVC contracts. They lay out in simple terms what DVC is, why it might make sense for you, and how much it costs. They are up front about all of the costs, both the initial buy-in cost and the recurring yearly maintenance fees. I've noticed that other timeshare presentations often try to mask or downplay the yearly recurring costs, but you need to be fully aware of them as they are substantial over the course of a contract.

At the end of the DVC presentation, the associates don't pressure you to buy in, they simply state that if you want to learn more you can talk with an associate one-on-one, or if you're not interested that's fine, too. Disney recognizes that DVC is not for everyone, and if DVC isn't for you they still want you to vacation at Disney, so they are not going to do anything to jeopardize the way you feel about their company by using high-pressure sales tactics.

While I recommend attending a DVC presentation if you are able, I still suggest caution: while their sales pitch is low pressure, they will typically throw out some special offers that will make it seem like you should buy in on the spot. The first time we attended a DVC presentation, they had a great offer that essentially would have given us a double dose of points for the first year of our membership. Luckily, we were able to contain our enthusiasm long enough to do our own research before jumping in, and ended up finding out that we could get essentially the same deal through a resale purchase (we'll get into resale purchases a little bit later in this book). Before you rush to sign that first DVC contract, it benefits you to sit down, take a deep breath, and ask yourself if DVC is right for you.

So how do you know if the Disney Vacation Club really *is* right for you? There are many factors to consider, but they fall into two broad categories: vacation habits and financial considerations.

Vacation habits are factors like how often do you visit Disney resorts, and what types of Disney accommodations do you typically like to stay at (value, moderate, or deluxe). Your past vacation habits are important to consider, but you should also think about how you'd want to vacation if you didn't have to think about financial consider-ations. For example, a common recommendation is that if you stay at Disney value resorts, DVC is not right for you. But that is not always the case. Do you stay at a Disney value resort because you want to, or because you have to (for financial reasons)? If you want to stay at a value resort, then it is true that DVC is probably not a great fit for you. But if you are staying at a value because you have to, but would really rather stay at a moderate or deluxe resort if you had the means, then DVC may be a viable option.

Let's dive a little deeper and take a look at how your frequency of Disney visits relates to being a good candidate to buy into DVC. The Disney Vacation Club is built for people who vacation at a Disney resort at least once every three years, so if you are an occasional visitor, I can tell you right off the bat that DVC is probably not a great fit for you. If you visit at least once every 1–3 years, or more, then it can be a great fit. In general, the more often you visit Walt Disney World, the better the DVC will work for you.

Now, you may be asking why I specify vacations at Walt Disney World when there are DVC resorts elsewhere as well. The reason is simple: most DVC resorts are at Walt Disney World, and while you can exchange your points for a non-DVC timeshare vacation at many other destinations around the world, the real reason you'd want to buy into DVC is to stay at Walt Disney World because that's where you get the most vacation value as a DVC member—not only in terms of points, but also in terms of discounts and room options.

You may also wonder why I say DVC is a good fit if you visit WDW at least every 1–3 years. The flexibility of DVC allows you to use up to 3 years of points in one shot. This is done by what's called "banking" and "borrowing" your points. Throughout this book I'm going to use the fictional Parr family to give some examples to help you better understand the ins and outs of DVC. If you're a Disney/Pixar fan, you may be familiar with the "Incredible" Parr family which consists of parents Bob and Helen, as well as their children Violet, Dash, and baby Jack-Jack. Let's take a look at how the Parr family could use the banking and borrowing features of their DVC contract:

> Bob and Helen Parr have a smaller-than-average DVC contract of 125 vacation points. Bob's use year has arrived, so he just received his yearly allotment of points, but he knows he and his superhero family are not going to use those points this year, because he doesn't have any vacation time (fighting villains is a 24-hour per day job!). What Bob can do is bank all 125 of this year's points to his next use year.
>
> One year later and Bob has a double-dose of points (250 points) to use. He wants to plan a really magical vacation for his family, and maybe take some extra friends or family along. Bob can use all 250 of his points, or if he needs even more points, he can borrow all of his points from the next use year, giving him 3 years of points for one trip—that's 375 points!

> *With 375 points, Bob has a lot of options. He can book a luxurious week-long stay in a two-bedroom, 1230-square-foot villa at Walt Disney World's flagship resort, the Grand Floridian. And while the Grand Floridian is incredible, Bob could even opt for a roomier accommodation like a three-bedroom, 2400-square-foot villa at Disney's Old Key West Resort.*
>
> *So, with Bob's small 125-point contract, he can book a big vacation by using 3 years of points in one shot!*

The banking and borrowing features of DVC allow you to leverage your points for whatever situation works best for you. We'll talk more in subsequent chapters about how many points you'll need and what the term "use year" means, but the 125-point contract we looked at as an example is slightly less than an average DVC contract, which fall in the 150–160 point range.

Now that we've looked at how often you visit, let's take a more in depth look at how the type of resort where you want to stay affects whether or not DVC is right for you. Again, you need to consider the type of resort you *want* to stay at. I stayed at value resorts not because I necessarily wanted to, but more out of necessity—before my wife and I became a DVC members we just couldn't afford to go as often as we wanted while also staying at a moderate or deluxe. Don't get me wrong. The value resorts are very nice and I would take them any day compared to staying off Disney property. If you are perfectly happy staying at a value resort like an All-Star, Pop Century, or Art of Animation, then DVC is not a great fit. If you like to stay in moderate or deluxe hotels, however, DVC will save you money in the long run.

Another consideration is the size of your family. Standard rooms at the value resorts can only accommodate four people, if you have a family of five or more you will either need to book a family suite at the value resorts or move up to a five-person room at a moderate resort (which is usually cheaper than a value family suite). This was the case with our family. When we had two children we had no problem with staying at a value resort. Then, along came our third child, and the realization that we could no longer fit in a standard value room, so we started staying at Port Orleans Riverside. While we had been happy with a value, once we tried a moderate resort we found that we really liked it and couldn't imagine going back to a value. When we found out that several DVC resorts accommodate up to five guests in a studio (as of this writing: Grand Floridian, Polynesian, and Wilderness Lodge; upcoming renovations at the Beach Club and Boardwalk resorts will bring their studio capacity up to five as well), it was a big factor in us taking the plunge in DVC. Just as had been the case when we started staying in a moderate resort and couldn't imagine going back to a value, once we stayed in a DVC villa, we didn't want to go back to a moderate!

Now that we've taken a look at vacationing habits, let's turn to financial considerations when deciding whether or not to buy into DVC. It's hard to argue that financial considerations are not the most important drivers for deciding whether or not to purchase DVC. Financial considerations deal with determining the total cost of ownership, return on investment, how you will pay to buy into DVC, and whether or not you can afford both the up-front cost and the recurring fees.

Let's first look at total cost of ownership. When you buy into DVC, you pay a lump sum based on the amount of points you want, plus closing costs. So, once you buy in you won't have any more recurring costs to worry about, right? Unfortunately, this is not the case. There are also yearly maintenance fees to consider. These fees go toward paying for things like upkeep of the resort, similar to an HOA for your house or condo. The amount of these fees is dependent on which DVC resort is your home resort (we'll get into home resorts in the next chapter) and how many points you have. For example, Saratoga Springs has a maintenance fee of \$5.1749/pt. If you have an average-sized contract of 150 points, your yearly maintenance fees will be \$776.24. Keep in mind also that maintenance fees do typically increase each year, and some resorts have higher maintenance fees than others, so this will be an important factor in choosing a home resort.

Many people don't budget properly for maintenance fees and are caught by surprise when they come due. I recommend putting a little bit aside each week or month so the money is there when you need it. My wife and I put aside a set amount from our paychecks each week to cover DVC maintenance fees; it's nice to have that money ready and waiting each year when you need it. Disney also lets you pay your maintenance fees on a monthly basis for no extra charge.

Below is a list of maintenance fee rates each DVC resort for 2015:

Resort	Point Cost
Animal Kingdom Villas	$6.2989
Aulani	$6.5100
Bay Lake Tower	$5.0504
Beach Club Villas	$5.9748
Boardwalk Villas	$6.0735
Grand Californian	$5.1483
Grand Floridian	$5.5216
Hilton Head	$6.5190
Old Key West	$5.8370
Polynesian	$6.0251
Saratoga Springs	$5.1749
Vero Beach	$8.0600
Wilderness Lodge	$6.0251

The last financial consideration is determining how you will pay to buy into DVC, This is obviously a personal choice based on your finances. I recommend only buying into DVC if you have the money to do so. I like to dissuade people from financing their DVC purchase, though I realize that coming up with the cash to buy in is not always an option. If you buy directly from Disney, they do offer financing; typically, the term for a DVC loan is 10 years.

When determining the return on investment of a DVC purchase, there are several things to consider. First, the points required to book DVC rooms never change, so you are locking in your price for the next 40–50 years (depending on your contract length). Second, you will have access to *many* discounts, including 10% on all merchandise at WDW, 10%–20% at select dining locations, discounted pricing on annual passes, eligibility for the Tables in Wonderland dining discount card, and special promotions and member-exclusive experiences. Plus, you'll be able to rent your points out if you aren't going to use them. We'll look at some financial analysis examples in the next chapter.

Something else you may want to consider prior to joining the Disney Vacation Club is your age—will you be able to fully use the 50-year contract? Let me first be very clear—if you are a senior and believe that DVC is right for you based on the factors we've discussed in the previous paragraphs, I encourage you to buy into DVC and enjoy your membership. The great thing about DVC is you can use your points to book some great extended family vacations and share the Disney magic with your kids and/or grandkids. I can guarantee you the memories you make together will be priceless. Even if you expect that you may not outlive your DVC contract, you have the option of willing it to your children. I'm sure your kids would be thrilled to inherit a DVC membership and continue to create new and lasting memories.

We've covered quite a bit in this chapter, and your head might be spinning. I know that it can be a lot to take in and DVC can be confusing. In order to make it a little bit easier for you to decide whether or not to buy into the Disney Vacation Club, I've compiled a list of basic questions that you can ask yourself to determine if DVC is right for you. If you answer NO to any of these questions, then DVC is probably not a good fit; but, if you can answer YES or even MAYBE to all of them, then I encourage you to get started today.

- Do you visit Walt Disney World at least once every 1–3 years?
- Do you want to stay at moderate or deluxe Disney resorts, or have more than four people in your family?
- Can you afford to buy into the Disney Vacation Club (typically $10k–$20k for an average contract)?
- Can you afford the yearly maintenance fees (typically $750/year for an average 150-point contract)?
- Can you benefit from the many DVC discounts that you would have access to?

The rest of this book will deal with the nitty-gritty details of how to buy a DVC contract in the most economical manner and how to get the absolute most out of it.

THREE

Getting Started

Walt Disney once said "The way to get started is to quit talking and begin doing". Many of us talk about doing something and don't act, or complain about something but don't take any steps to change it. If, after reading the previous chapter, you've determined that DVC is right for you, it's now time to take action.

So how do you get started?

The first step in getting started with the DVC purchasing process is to determine the best method for buying in. When I first started researching DVC, I thought the only way to purchase a DVC contract was directly through Disney. While that is certainly the quickest and easiest method, there's another less expensive method out there that you may not even be aware of: the resale market.

Resale is an excellent option that many people overlook. It's a great way to minimize your up-front costs. Once your purchase is complete, your recurring costs will be the same whether you chose a direct purchase or resale purchase. While the initial buy-in cost is the biggest advantage to buying resale, another nice aspect is that you can find a contract that works the best for you in terms of home resort and amount of points, as well as use year (use year is a somewhat confusing term; it refers to the month in which you receive your points each year). We bought our first DVC contract through resale and it allowed us to buy in at less than half of what it would have cost us directly from Disney, and we were even able to get a little bit larger contract than we would have been able to get through a direct purchase.

While resale was a great option for us, it isn't for everybody. The biggest downside to resale purchases is the amount of time it takes to complete a transaction. The resale buying process often takes around 2–3 months from offer to closing, while buying from Disney is pretty much an instantaneous deal. Another disadvantage is that your contract length will be shorter. Typically, direct purchase contracts expire about 50 years from the date that sales opened for each home resort. Resale contracts will have a shorter term. For example, if you buy into the Grand Floridian Resort, your contract expires in 2064, which is 50 years after the DVC section of the resort opened in 2013. If you buy a resale contract at Saratoga Springs, your contract would expire in 2054 because that resort opened in 2004. So, if somebody bought into Saratoga Springs in 2004 and then decided to sell it on the resale market in 2014, the contract would only have 40 years left on it.

To help you decide the best route for you to buy into DVC, I've compiled the following list of resale pros and cons:

Pros:

- Much lower buy-in cost.
- You can negotiate the sale price and whether buyer or seller pays the closing costs.
- Sometimes you can find contracts that have banked points from a previous use year, so you can start with a double dose of points.
- More resort choices—this is great for keeping your yearly maintenance fees low.
- Choice of use year.

Cons:

- Lengthy process (3 months or more).
- Disney has what's called "right of first refusal" (ROFR) on resale contracts, which means they can buy the contract out from under you during the process, and you'll have to start over (in chapter 3 we'll discuss ROFR in more detail and suggest ways to avoid it).
- You won't be able to use your points to book resorts in the Disney Collection (non-DVC Disney resorts & Disney Cruise Line) or Concierge Collection. This was a change made in 2011 by Disney to try and sway people toward buying directly from them instead of resale. As a resale buyer, you will still have access to all DVC resorts and the World Collection. In reality, using your DVC points on the Disney Collection or Concierge Collection is not a very good use of your points anyhow, since the points required to book these are astronomical.

In chapter 4 we will take an in-depth look at buying into DVC via the resale market, but for the remainder of this chapter let's assume that you are buying directly from Disney.

Once you decide your buy-in method, the next decision you will need to make is to choose a home resort. What does your home resort mean? Does it mean that it's the only resort where you can stay? Absolutely not. There are two things your home resort affects: your booking window and your maintenance fees. You will be able to book your home resort up to eleven months in advance of your stay, while all other DVC resorts will have a booking window of seven months. Your home resort also determines how much your yearly maintenance fees cost and when your contract expires.

Below is a list of opening and expiration years for each DVC resort:

Resort	Open/Expire
Polynesian	2015/2066
Grand Floridian	2013/2064
Aulani	2011/2062
Bay Lake Tower	2009/2060
Grand Californian	2009/2060
Animal Kingdom	2007/2057
Saratoga Springs	2004/2054
Beach Club Villas	2002/2042
Wilderness Lodge	2000/2042
Boardwalk Villas	1996/2042
Hilton Head	1996/2042
Vero Beach	1995/2042
Old Key West	1991/2042

Disney will typically offer the newest Vacation Club resorts for direct purchases (currently, Disney's Polynesian Villas and Grand Floridian Villas in Walt Disney World, and Disney's Aulani resort in Hawaii). While not advertised, Disney does allow you to buy into older DVC resorts if you so desire, but they have a limited number of these and surprisingly they aren't really that much cheaper than the newest resorts, so for direct purchases it benefits you to go with the new resorts where you will typically end up with a 50-year contract. Disney will also have promotions quite often on the new resorts to sweeten the deal even more. If you want to buy into an older DVC resort, I recommend pursuing a resale contract.

To calculate how many points you will need, determine how frequently you plan to visit a DVC resort, the length of a typical visit, during which season you will typically visit, which DVC resort you want to stay at most of the time, and what type of room you want to stay in.

Figuring out frequency and length of visits is pretty self-explanatory, but which season you visit has a big impact on how many points you'll need. For example, if you visit during slow periods like January and September, you will need fewer points than if you stayed at a busier time like Christmas or Spring Break. You may think that figuring out which resort to stay at will just be your home resort, and that may be the case for some folks, but you aren't stuck staying there—you can stay at any of the DVC resorts, provided there is availability.

Most DVC resorts have four types of rooms, each requiring more points as you move up the chain (deluxe studio, one-bedroom villa, two-bedroom villa, and three-bedroom grand villa). Not all room types are offered at every resort, and some resorts have unique room types, such as the Treehouse Villas at Saratoga Springs or the Bora Bora Over-the-Water Bungalows at Disney's Polynesian Resort. Each resort has its own points chart that will show costs for each room type and season. Some resorts also have multiple view types that you can choose from.

In our previous example, we used Bob Parr to illustrate how a DVC member could use three years of points on one vacation. In that example, Bob and his family had a 125-point contract. Here they are again, in a different situation:

> Bob and Helen Parr plan to visit Walt Disney World once each year in October, for a week, and stay at the Grand Floridian. Looking at the Grand Floridian's points chart, we see that the resort has five different seasons: Adventure, Choice, Dream, Magic, and Premier. The whole month of October falls within the Choice Season, which is the second lowest cost season. Bob and Helen have three "Incredible" children, so they will need a room that accommodates at least five guests. Luckily, the Grand Floridian is one of the DVC resorts that does allow

up to five guests in a studio. They could also opt for a one-bedroom (247 points), a two-bedroom (340 points), or even a three-bedroom grand villa for 824 points. Bob and Helen want to use their points as efficiently as possible; in fact, Helen really likes to "stretch" their DVC points as far as they can possibly go, so they decide to stick with a deluxe studio room. Some DVC resorts offer different views, and the Grand Floridian is one of those—a standard studio is 125 points for the week and a lake-view studio is 153 points per week during the Choice Season. Again, Bob and Helen want to keep costs down, so they decide that a 125 point contract will be perfect for them.

While our example used a week-long trip to figure out the points requirements, you don't have to buy week-long chunks as is the case with many timeshares. The flexibility of the Disney Vacation Club allows you to pick whatever days you would like as long as there's availability. A standard-view deluxe studio at the Grand Floridian will cost you 17 points for a weekday (Sunday through Thursday) and 20 points for a weekend (Friday and Saturday) during the Choice Season. So, if you wanted a five night stay, you could buy a 91-point contract (two weekend nights and three weekday nights), or just make it an even 100 points to give you a little padding.

Typically, the minimum purchase for first-time DVC members buying directly from Disney is 100 points, although I have heard Disney may make exceptions to this rule. While most choose a typical DVC contract value like 50, 100, 125, 150, etc., when you buy directly through Disney you can opt for whatever points amount best suits your vacation needs. Existing DVC members can purchase add-on contracts for as little as 25 points. These add-on contracts do not have to be at the same home resort. DVC members can have multiple home resorts; however, if you are using your points to book a trip within the 11-month home resort booking window, you need to have enough points in that contract to do so.

Another consideration when purchasing DVC points is whether or not you may need to sell them at some point down the road. I know this may seem inconceivable, but the fact is that sometimes life happens and you need emergency money, and your DVC contract is an asset that you can sell if you need to. Generally, smaller contracts (less than 200 points) are easier to sell than large ones, so you're better off having multiple small contracts rather than one large contract.

Now that you've determined how many DVC points you will need and what resort you want to buy into, it's time to take a look at the total cost for your DVC membership. Remember that there are two costs to consider with any DVC contract: the buy-in cost and recurring costs. With that in mind, let's use the Parrs again as an example to walk-through the financial analysis of a DVC contract:

Bob and Helen Parr decided earlier that they wanted to purchase a 125-point contract at Disney's Grand Floridian Resort. Disney is currently charging $165 per point, so in order to figure out their buy-in cost they would simply multiply this by the number of points they are purchasing:

Points Purchase = $165/point * 125 points = $20,625

While maintenance fees are a yearly recurring cost, Disney will also want Bob and Helen to pay maintenance fees up front for the first year of their DVC contract. The current maintenance fee rate at Disney's Grand Floridian Resort is $5.5216 per point, so we multiply this figure by the total number of points:

Maintenance Fee = $5.5216/point * 125 points = $690.20

The final part of finding Bob and Helen's total buy-in cost is adding in the closing costs, which will typically run about $500 for this size contract. Bob and Helen can find their total buy-in cost by adding the points purchase, first-year's maintenance fee, and closing costs:

Total buy-in cost = $20,625 + $690.20 + $500 = $21,815.20

Now that the Parrs know how much it will cost to purchase their contract, they also want to know how much their contract will cost them every year. The maintenance fees that were calculated above are a recurring yearly cost. Bob and Helen need to remember a couple of things about maintenance fees. First, the maintenance fee rate will typically increase every year, usually by 3–5%. Secondly, Bob and Helen can choose how they pay their maintenance fees—either in one lump sum or as a monthly payment.

The next area the Parrs want to look at is the total cost of ownership over the life of their DVC contract. Disney Vacation Club contracts are 50 years in length; however, the 50 years starts when the resort opens, so if you buy one year after the resort opens, your contract will have 49 years remaining. For simplicity's sake, let's assume a 50-year contract for Bob and Helen. To find the total cost, we simply multiply the length of the contract minus one year by the yearly maintenance fee (remember that Bob and Helen already paid for the first year of maintenance fees when they bought into DVC), then add the total buy-in cost:

DVC 50-year cost = 49 years * $690.20/year + $21,815.20 = $55,635

In reality, the total cost will be more because maintenance fees increase each year, but we don't know for sure how much the maintenance fees will increase, so in order to simplify this analysis and compare it to the cost of regular resort stays, we're taking inflation out of the equation and looking at everything in today's dollars.

A total lifetime cost of $55,635 seems like an awful lot of money for Bob and Helen, but let's take a look at how much it would cost for weekly stays at a Disney Resort over a 50-year span, starting with the value resorts. A weeklong stay in a standard room at a value resort in October would cost Bob and Helen about $985. We multiply this by 50 years to find the total cost:

Value resort 50-year cost = 50 years * $985/year = $49,250

This figure is less than the 50-year cost of a DVC membership, which is in line with what we stated earlier, that if you stay at Disney value resorts, DVC is not a great fit for you. But remember, Bob and Helen Parr have 3 children, so a standard room at a value resort, which only accommodates up to four guests, would not be an option for them. The Parrs would have to move up to either a family suite at a value resort, or stay at a moderate resort like Port Orleans Riverside that can accommodate 5 guests in a standard room.

A standard room at Port Orleans Riverside would be cheaper, so let's explore that option. A weeklong stay in a standard room at Port Orleans in October will cost Bob and Helen $2,360. To find the total equivalent cost, we would multiply this by 50 years:

Moderate resort 50-year cost = 50 years * $2,360/year = $118,000

Now Bob and Helen are starting to see the money-saving power of the Disney Vacation Club! Buying into the DVC would cost much less than yearly cash stays at a moderate resort; over $62,000 less, in fact—that's a savings of over 50%.

Let's not forget, however, that DVC resorts are considered deluxe resorts, not moderates. So, if Bob and Helen really want to look at an "apples-to-apples" comparison, they should be looking at how *much it would cost to stay at a deluxe resort. And not just any Deluxe Resort: let's use their home resort as an example for a true comparison. A week-long stay in a standard room at Disney's Grand Floridian in October will cost the Parrs $4,480. Over 50 years that amounts to:*

Deluxe resort 50-year cost = 50 * $4,480 = $224,000

Buying into DVC will save the Parrs over $168,000 compared to staying on a cash reservation at Disney's Grand Floridian each year. That's a savings of over 75%. Talk about incredible!!

Again, this is a simple analysis that does not take into account inflation. You can count on maintenance fees increasing every year, but the cost of non-DVC Disney hotel rooms will do the same thing (and probably at a faster rate).

The financial analysis we've just explored is somewhat conservative in the sense that it doesn't take into account all of the savings and discounts that you'll enjoy as a DVC member, such as 10% merchandise discounts as well as various dining discounts. These discounts can be quite substantial and can mean that your break-even point with a DVC purchase happens much sooner. I didn't include these discounts, because there is no guarantee that they will always be there. Discounts are always subject to change, so I prefer to leave them out of the financial analysis, just to be conservative. Nevertheless, the perks and discounts that you will enjoy are pretty substantial, so we will devote an entire chapter of this book just to those things.

FOUR

Buying Resale

While it's nice to buy new things, buying used can save you a lot of money. Regardless of your income, it's safe to say that everybody likes to save a little money. In fact, most millionaires gained their wealth not by spending lavishly, but by saving their money and investing it wisely. One of the best lessons my father taught me was how to save money and spend it wisely. Growing up, I always had one job or another—mowing lawns, delivering newspapers, etc. By the time I was a teenager I had enough money to buy my own car, and my dad made a deal with me—he promised that if I bought my own car and took care of maintaining it properly, he would pay the insurance on it (which was really a great deal if you consider the cost of insuring a teenage driver). I bought my own car at the age of 14 for $2500 and spent the next 2 years fixing it up while waiting to get my driver's license. It was a great car, but by the time I was midway through college I was ready for something a little nicer. I had a great paying internship and I was so excited to finally be making "real money". I went out and started looking at new cars—they were really nice, but also really expensive. My dad had always bought used cars, so I started looking at those and found a great deal on a car that was less than two years old and had low mileage. The lesson I learned was that while new cars are nice, slightly used cars were also nice—and much cheaper! The same principles can be applied to purchasing a DVC contract.

While Disney may refer to the Disney Vacation Club as its best-kept secret, I think buying DVC through the resale market is an even better-kept secret. Not many people even realize that this is an option for them. I know it took me awhile to realize it! While resale is a good option to save on the initial buy-in cost, it can be a lengthy process and you may hit some road bumps along the way.

The biggest thing that can scare people away from resale is what's called ROFR (right-of-first refusal). Essentially, Disney has the right to buy a contract out from under you during the resale process if they think the price is too low. Disney has a 30-day period to do this, and they typically take that entire 30 days or close to it. But the financial benefits are worth the wait, and in reality Disney does not exercise ROFR on many contracts.

So, how do you get started with finding and buying a DVC contract on the resale market? First you're going to have to determine what resort you want to buy into and how many points you want, just as we discussed in the previous chapter. In terms of resorts, you'll want to balance a few things here. If staying at one particular resort is important to you, then choose that resort as your home resort so you get the benefit of being able to book eleven months out instead of seven. If you are happy with any DVC resort, I recommend you balance maintenance fee cost, buy-in cost, and the length of the contract. For example, Saratoga Springs is usually a good choice as it has one of the lowest resale buy-in costs of all DVC resorts, the second lowest maintenance fee cost, and the contract doesn't expire until 2054. Contrast this with the Beach Club or Wilderness Lodge resorts which have a higher buy-in cost, higher maintenance fees, and expire in 2042. Remember, just because a DVC resort is not your home resort doesn't mean you can't stay there; it just may be a little more difficult to get a reservation, depending on what time of the year you visit.

You will also want to consider choosing the right "use year". To review, use year refers to the month in which you'll receive your points each year (on the first of the month). You'll want your use year to be eight months or less before your vacation. Why eight months? We'll get into the details of that in the "Using DVC" chapter, but it is basically so that in the event of a cancellation you will have time to bank your points to the following use year before the banking deadline

Once you've figured out how many points you want, which home resort you want to target, and a use year that best suits your vacation needs, it's time to start looking online for resale listings. This is where you will want to be careful of where you search. Some agents are easier to work than others, and this will directly affect how your buying experience goes. One agency that I like and have personally used is Fidelity Resales. Fidelity deals with both Disney timeshares and other timeshares. There are a few more resale agencies that specialize primarily or exclusively in DVC properties, such as ResalesDVC. You will want to browse their website listings and see what they have available. You may also consider contacting the agency and letting them know what you are looking for so they can help you find it—sometimes they have new listings that haven't gone up on the website yet. Keep in mind as you browse the listings that the price per point that you pay is negotiable with the seller, as are closing costs, so don't get too hung up on the price. Some sellers are more motivated than others. You will also want to pay attention to how many points the contract has available for the current use year; sometimes you can find a contract that has points banked from the previous year, which is a nice bonus.

Once you have found a listing that you like, it's time to make an offer. I recommend visiting sites like MouseOwners.com or DISBoards.com, as they have forums discussing the average price that resale contracts are going for. Not all contracts are the same, so you have to be careful here. For example, some contracts may have points that have been banked from previous years, meaning you'll have plenty of points to use right away—these types of contracts will be worth a premium compared to other contracts that have no banked points, no current use year points, or even those that may have had points borrowed from future use years, meaning you'll have to wait awhile to actually use your contract. If you make your offer too low and the seller accepts your offer, you may be excited to have found a great deal, but you run the risk of having Disney exercise ROFR on the contract. If this happens, you will have to start the process all over again with a different contract. You will also have to negotiate who pays the closing costs (you or the seller), and who pays the current year's maintenance fees. I recommend trying to have the seller pay all of the closing costs, or at least a portion of them. However, I also recommend that you as the buyer pay the current year's maintenance fees, as this will lower your chances of having Disney exercise ROFR on your contract. You may end up going back and forth with the seller a few times before you agree on a price. This is where having a great agent really helps, as they will help to move the process along. Sometimes sellers can be a little bit slow in responding to an offer, and things like this can draw out the process unless you have an agent who really stays on top of things. Don't be afraid to keep in touch with the agent during this process; remember, the agent is working for you. Once you agree on a price and terms, your agent will write up an official contract. Writing up the contract will usually take 2–3 days, sometimes longer if several drafts need to be written until both you and the seller agree on the wording. Make sure the contract is written up correctly and don't be afraid to have your agent correct anything you don't like; this is a large purchase and you'll want to make sure it's correct.

One aspect of buying a resale DVC contract that you'll want to consider is if you want the seller to bank any points from the current use year. For example, let's consider a contract with a use year of December (remember that use year is the month that you receive your points each year). It's currently July and the contract you are trying to buy has 100 points left on the current use year. You don't plan to use any of those 100 points during the current use year. DVC points must be banked within the first 8 months of the use year or you will lose them, so in this case the points must be banked by July 31. In case your purchase doesn't close prior to July 31, you may want to stipulate in the contract that the seller will bank those points so that you do not lose them. This was an opportunity that we missed out on with our first DVC contract because we simply didn't know about the banking deadline—we assumed that we could bank points until the end of the use year. Luckily, in our case, Disney was nice enough to make an exception and let us bank those points anyway. DVC member services did make it very clear to us that it was a one-time exception since we were buying in, and that in the future they would not make any exceptions to the banking deadline. Once your contract is acceptable to all parties, you'll be required to put down a deposit to be held in escrow—typically $1000. Depending on the agent you are using, you may have the option of charging the deposit to a credit card, which will speed up the process compared to writing a check and mailing it in.

After you sign your contract and send in the deposit check or pay the deposit by credit card, your agent will have the sellers sign the contract. Once the contract is signed by both parties and the escrow amount is paid, your agent will send it to Disney to begin the ROFR process. Disney has 30 days to exercise ROFR and they will typically take that entire amount of time, or at least three of the four weeks. I think this is probably the worst part of the process—it is an agonizing wait, during which time you will be debating whether or not your offer was good enough to pass. It's easy to second guess yourself, but be patient and let the process play out. It does seem that Disney typically does not exercise ROFR on contracts from first-time buyers unless the price-per-point is much, much lower than they think it should be. The main reason for ROFR is to maintain the value of DVC contracts; while it is an agonizing process, in the long run as a future DVC owner it does benefit you as it ensures that the resale market is not too low. It can be difficult to avoid calling your agent every day to check if you passed ROFR. I told myself at the outset of the process that I wasn't going to be one of those people, but by week three I couldn't take it anymore and started calling him. Luckily, about two days after contacting my agent, he got an answer from Disney and we passed ROFR on our first DVC contract.

Your agent will contact you when Disney makes a decision on ROFR. If your contract makes it through ROFR, the agent will then send everything to the closing company and you will typically receive closing documents to sign in about 7–10 days. You will need to send in the signed closing documents, along with the final payment, to the closing agent. The seller must also sign the documents and send them back to the closing agent. The closing process can be drawn out if either you or the seller are slow in getting everything signed and returned, but usually both parties are motivated to get the process done as soon as possible—you, as the buyer, want your contract so that you can start to use it, and the seller wants their money. Much of the closing can be done by faxing the documents back and forth, or scanning/emailing, to expedite the process. After the closing company receives everything from both you and the seller, they will notify DVC of the contract transfer and send the documents to the country clerk for recording of the deed. The total closing process typically takes about 2–3 weeks from passing ROFR to recording of the deed. If you really want to stay on top of things, you can visit the Orange County, Florida, recorders website to search for deeds to see when yours is recorded! It's pretty cool to see the official deed showing that you are, in fact, a DVC member and own a real estate interest in the most magical place on earth!

You will receive a welcome packet from Disney with your DVC membership number in 7–10 days after the deed is recorded. This is probably the most exciting part of the process, as you will finally feel like an official DVC member. You will also receive membership cards, although these sometimes arrive later in a separate package. Once you have your membership number, you can call DVC member services to set up your online account and start making reservations.

Overall, the entire resale process takes 2–3 months, depending on how fast your agent is and how responsive the sellers are in signing everything promptly. While this may seem like a long time compared to a direct purchase where you will receive your points right away, you could save up to 50% or more on the initial buy-in cost.

While buying resale is going to save you a ton of money, it is still a large purchase. I recommend that you don't buy in unless you can pay cash. It is a little more difficult to get financing on a resale purchase compared to a direct purchase from Disney, but your agent can work with you to find financing. Let's use Bob and Helen Parr again to walk through a financial analysis of buying a DVC resale contract, and contrast it with our previous direct-purchase example:

After learning about DVC, Bob and Helen did some more research and decided they wanted to buy a resale contract. They had already decided that they needed at least 125 points, but after seeing the prices of resale contracts. they chose to aim a little higher and find something with 150–160 points. The Parrs targeted Saratoga Springs as their home resort because of the low price-per-point cost and low maintenance fees. They found a 150-point contract with a September use year, which was perfect for them since Bob and Helen usually stay at Walt Disney World in October. The contract they were targeting was $75/point and had 300 points available for the current use year because the sellers had banked all 150 of their points from the last use year. After researching the current market using the forums at MouseOwners.com, Bob and Helen contacted the resale agent and put in an offer of $68/point with the sellers paying the closing costs. The sellers countered at $70/point, and Bob and Helen agreed. Their sales agent wrote up the contract, and the Parrs signed it and sent in their escrow money.

Let's look at how much it will cost Bob and Helen. We take the $70 per point price that was agreed upon and multiply it by the number of points:

Points purchase = $70/point * 150 points = $10,500

Similar to a direct purchase from Disney, Bob and Helen must still pay maintenance fees for the first contract year. But remember, this resale contract that the Parrs are buying is a Saratoga Springs contract, so the maintenance fee rate is different than that of the Grand Floridian. The current maintenance fee rate at Disney's Saratoga Springs Resort is $5.1749 per point, so we multiply this figure by the total number of points:

Maintenance fee = $5.1749/point * 150 points = $776.24

The final part of the total buy-in cost for a resale contract is closing costs, which will still run about $500 for this size contract. Now we can find the total buy-in cost for Bob and Helen's resale contract by adding the points purchase, first-year's maintenance fee, and closing costs

Total buy-in cost = $10,500 + $776 + $500 = $11,776.24

At this point, Bob and Helen can hardly believe their eyes; this resale contract is cheaper than the direct-purchase contract at the Grand Floridian, which would have been $21,815.20. The contract is nearly 50% less than direct purchase, and it has more points! Bob and Helen do take note that their yearly maintenance fees are more expensive, but only because this contract has 25 more points than the direct-purchase contract, not because the maintenance fee rate is more. Remember that Disney's Saratoga Springs Resort is 10 years older than the Grand Floridian DVC Resort, which means 10 less years on the contract, so the Parrs want to see what the total cost is and how it compares to a cash stay at each resort level. To find the total cost over the length of the contract, we simply multiply the length of the contract minus one year by the yearly maintenance fee (remember that Bob and Helen already paid for the first year of maintenance fees when they bought into DVC), then add the total buy-in cost:

DVC 40-year cost = 39 years * $776.24/year + $11,776.24 = $42,049.60

In reality, the total cost will be more because maintenance fees increase each year, but in order to simplify this analysis and compare it to a regular resort stay, we're taking inflation out of the equation and looking at everything in today's dollars. A total lifetime cost of $42,049.60 seems pretty good compared to the direct purchase contract at the Grand Floridian that would have been $55,000.

Let's take a look at how much it would cost for weekly stays at a Disney resort over a 40-year span, first at a value resort. A weeklong *stay in a standard room in October would cost Bob and Helen Parr about $985. We multiply this by 40 years to find the total cost:*

Value resort 40-year cost = 40 years * $985/year = $39,360

This figure is still less than the 40-year cost of a DVC membership, but the difference is much closer than it was with the direct purchase example. When the Parrs take into account the discounts and perks they will receive as DVC members, they may still end up saving money with DVC.

Now let's look at a moderate resort stay. A weeklong stay in a standard room at Port Orleans in October will cost the Parrs $2,360. We multiply this by 40 years to find the total cost:

Moderate resort 40-year cost = 40 years * $2,360/year = $94,400

Buying a resale DVC contract would cost much less than yearly cash stays at a moderate resort; over $50,000 less, in fact—that's a savings well over 50%!

As with our direct-purchase example, let's finally take a look at a cash reservation in a deluxe resort for a more "apples-to-apples" comparison. We'll again use Bob and Helen's home resort as an example, which will be Disney's Saratoga Springs Resort & Spa with their resale contract. A week-long stay in a standard deluxe studio room at Saratoga Springs in October will cost the Parr family $3,900. Over 40 years that amounts to:

Deluxe resort 40-year cost = 40 * $3,900 = $156,000

Buying into DVC will save the Parrs over $150,000 compared to staying on a cash reservation at Saratoga Springs each year. That's a savings of over 70% for Bob and Helen Parr.

Bob and Helen decide to purchase the 150-point resale contract instead of the 125-point direct from Disney contract.

Like our direct purchase example, this is also a simple analysis that does not take into account inflation—DVC maintenance fees will increase year over year, as will the cost of non-DVC hotel rooms. But the analysis does show the power of a resale purchase, especially in terms of initial buy-in cost. This example has more points than our direct purchase example, but is almost half the cost. The maintenance fee rate at Saratoga Springs is also less than the Grand Floridian. Keep in mind that the price per point is negotiable on resale contracts, so while this example shows $70/point, it could be less, and you can even ask the seller to pay the closing costs.

Remember from earlier in this book when we talked about the importance of choosing the right use year? Let's use Bob and Helen Parr to show once again how picking the right use year can benefit you:

> *Bob and Helen vacation at Walt Disney World each year in October. The Parrs are looking for a resale contract and want to choose one that has a use year that will work for them. There are two contracts for sale that they like. Both are 150 points, one has a use year of September, and the other has a use year of January. The Parrs decide on the January use year because the sellers are asking $1 per point less than the September contract is listed for.*

> *A couple of years later, the Parrs need to cancel their October trip in September due to a change in Bob's schedule. It is September when they cancel, so they are already past the 8-month banking deadline (end of July for a January use year). Since they can't bank their points, they either have to use them by the end of the year or try to rent them out; otherwise, they will lose those points. They would have been better off going with the September use year even though the contract was more expensive. In reality, it wasn't that much more expensive—it was $1 per point more than the contract they bought; that's only $150!*

This example shows how sometimes, when buying a resale contract, we can get so caught up in the price per point that the seller is asking without considering other important factors.

One myth I've recently heard regarding resale contracts that I want to dispel is that Disney won't look at you as a "real" DVC member. This is false. Disney does not treat you any differently—you still receive all of the discounts that every other DVC member receives. Still, there are some restrictions on how you can use your DVC points. If you are using points to book DVC resorts, there is no difference. You can't, however, use your points to book Disney cruises, non-DVC resorts at Disney World, or Adventures by Disney. While this may seem like a big drawback, if you look at how many points you would need to book each of these, it is not a very wise use of points. In fact, when attending a DVC presentation, most of the time they will point out that it is better to pay cash for a Disney cruise rather than use DVC points.

Let's look at a Disney Cruise example. Since owners of resale contracts can't book Disney cruises using points, we'll use Bob and Helen's direct-purchase contract as an example. Remember that it was a 125-point DVC contract at Disney's Grand Floridian. This is how many points a Disney cruise would cost the Parrs:

> Bob Parr wants to take his family on an "incredible" Disney cruise. Bob has his eye on a 4-night cruise on the Disney Dream. Remember that the Parrs like to travel in October, which is considered the "regular" season for a Disney cruise—the cheapest season. The Parrs want a room with a verandah, but decide that an ocean-view family stateroom is a better option because it requires fewer points.
>
> According to the Disney cruise points chart, it will cost 111 points each for Bob and Helen (adults), 80 points for Violet (age 13 and up), 76 points for Dash (age 6-12), and 48 points for Jack-Jack (2 and under), for a grand total of 426 points. Even if they saved 3 years' worth of points, they still wouldn't have enough for this cruise.
>
> Typically, the cash value of one point is about $12 (the price you could get if you rented out your DVC points to somebody else). We multiply this by the amount of points required to book a cruise to find the equivalent cash/points value:
>
> Cash value = 426 points * $12/point = $5,112
>
> To give you an idea of the points vs. cash cost for a Disney cruise, a cash reservation for the Parr family cruise would be about $3500, so you'd save over $1600 by booking a cash reservation instead of using your points.
>
> Disney cruises are NOT a wise use of points! The Parrs would be better off booking a cash reservation and combining it with a points stay at a DVC resort at Walt Disney World for a land and sea adventure.

I hope this chapter has helped you learn more about one of the hidden aspects of saving on the purchase of a DVC contract. It's a great option and the benefits far outweigh the drawbacks. Whenever I talk to people that are interested in DVC, I always encourage them to check out the resale market. The initial buy-in cost of DVC is usually the biggest factor holding people back from joining.

Now that we've looked at how to buy into the DVC, let's take a look at how to best use your contract.

FIVE

Using DVC

It's official, you're a DVC member—but now what? Now it's time to start enjoying your DVC membership!

One of the great things about owning DVC is that you can make a reservation without having to pay anything out of pocket when booking your trip. You can simply go to the DVC website, use the Resort Availability tool to lookup which resorts are open during the dates you want to go, and book your trip.

The Resort Availability tool is something that is fairly new and a welcome addition to the DVC website. Previously, members were required to search each resort individually, which was very time consuming.

We've touched upon this a little bit in earlier chapters, but as a DVC member it is important that you are aware of some key dates so that you can plan your vacations accordingly and use your points wisely.

Let's first discuss when you can make your reservation:

- If you are making a reservation at your home resort, you can book eleven months prior to your check-in date.

- If you are visiting any other DVC resort, you can book seven months prior to check in.

Let's imagine that you want to book a seven-night stay with a check in of December 15, 2016:

- If you are staying at your home resort, you can make your reservation 11 months out, which would be January 15, 2016.

- If you are staying at any other DVC resort, you can make your reservation seven months out, which would be on May 15, 2016.

The chart below outlines when you can make your reservation:

Check in	Home Resort	Other DVC Resorts
January	February	June
February	March	July
March	April	August
April	May	September
May	June	October
June	July	November
July	August	December
August	September	January
September	October	February
October	November	March
November	December	April
December	January	May

It is also important to note that that you can only book a maximum of seven nights on the day that your booking window opens. This can be a little bit confusing, so let's walk through another example using the Parr family:

> Bob and Helen Parr want to book an eight-night vacation at Disney's Beach Club. Remember that when we last visited the Parr family, they had just purchased a resale contract at Disney's Saratoga Springs, so Beach Club is not their home resort. Since Beach Club is not their home resort, their booking window doesn't open until seven months before the trip they want to book. They plan to book an eight-night stay with a check-in date of October 15, so their booking window opens on April 15. Bob and Helen know that online reservations open at 6:00am EST. Since they are in the Central time zone, they wake up bright and early on April 15 to make their reservation; however, on April 15, they are disappointed to find out that they can only make a reservation for the first seven nights of their eight-night stay. If they want to make a reservation for all eight nights, they would have to wait one more day and make their reservation for eight nights on April 16.

> The Beach Club resort is popular in October due to the Food & Wine Festival at Epcot, which is steps away from the Beach Club, so if Bob

and Helen wait one day there's a pretty good chance the first day of their trip will no longer be available. Luckily, Bob and Helen read this book and know a trick to get around the seven-day rule! On April 15, they go ahead and book the first seven nights of their trip. The following morning, on April 16, they call into DVC Member Services and ask them to add an eighth day.

Some may ask why they couldn't just book the eighth day online. The "booking window plus seven-days" rule only applies for trips with check-in dates within the booking window. The online system can't bypass that restriction to add one day—member services must do it manually.

Now Bob and Helen can start their countdown to a magical, eight-day Disney trip at the Beach Club!

While we used a stay at the Beach Club resort in October as an example, in reality it would be difficult to obtain this reservation unless Beach Club is your home resort. The Epcot resort area is very popular during Epcot's Food & Wine Festival in the fall.

No matter what time of year you are staying, booking your DVC trip as early as possible will assure that you have the best selection of DVC resorts. However, not everyone can book a trip seven or eleven months out, because they may not know their schedule. It can be difficult to get a reservation less than seven months out, but there are some tools that can help you out.

Waitlisting is a great booking tool available to DVC members. If you can't find availability for a particular DVC resort/room type for the dates you are planning to visit, you can place yourself on a waitlist, which means that as people cancel reservations, Disney will automatically fill those rooms if they have people on the waitlist. Disney fills the waitlists based on when you created your request, so the earlier you submit your waitlist, the better. You can have up to two waitlists at a time, and you can create the waitlist such that it will replace an existing reservation of your choosing if you so desire.

Split stays are another option you may want to consider if you are booking late and the resort you want isn't available for the entire time. A split stay simply refers to the practice of staying at two or more Disney resorts during your Walt Disney World stay. This idea is not unique to the Disney Vacation Club; you could do this with any resort stay, and Disney makes split stays very easy to do. Disney will move your luggage free of charge between Disney resorts, and transportation isn't a problem because of Disney's vast resort-wide transportation system. I will admit that before trying a split stay, I didn't think too much of the idea. I was surprised at how easy it was the first time we tried it. Being able to experience two different Disney resorts in one vacation is a treat, and it almost felt like two vacations in one. Now I will admit that split stays make for some extra work—while Disney will move your luggage, you will still be responsible for packing up your luggage before you leave the first resort.

Let's look at another example to see how using waitlists and split stays can help with late trip planning:

> *Bob and Helen Parr's resale DVC purchase took longer than they anticipated. They are now DVC members, but it is July and they want to book an October trip. You'll remember that with their 150-point contract they actually have 300 points available because the previous owners had banked all of last year's points. They have to at least use the 150 banked points this year because points can only be banked once and then you must "use them or lose them".*

> *The Parrs could opt to only use their banked points from last year, and bank this year's 150 points to next year. Instead, they want to book a week-long trip that includes Grandma and Grandpa Parr. They figure a two-bedroom villa would work best; that way, Bob and Helen can have one bedroom, Grandma and Grandpa Parr can have the second bedroom, and the kids can sleep on the fold out sofa or the extra bed in Grandma and Grandpa's room. With the two-bedroom they will have plenty of room to spread out and they can use the full kitchen to make their own meals and save a little bit on dining costs.*

> *Because their check-in date is only three months away, Bob and Helen figure they will probably have to target one of the larger DVC resorts like Saratoga Springs, Old Key West, or Animal Kingdom Lodge Kidani. They pull up their DVC account online and use the resort availability tool to see which resorts have availability during the time that they want to visit WDW. The Parrs are disappointed to find that not one single DVC resort has availability for all of the dates they need. Now, they could try for different dates, but their vacation is really built around their children's school schedule, so changing dates isn't an option. They do notice, however, that Saratoga Springs has a*

three-night block open at the beginning of their vacation, and Animal Kingdom Lodge Kidani has a two-night block open at the end of their vacation. They remember from reading this book that split stays are often a good option for late booking, so they book the two reservations.

But, what about the two nights in the middle of their trip that they are missing? That's where waitlists come into play!

Bob and Helen can use this great DVC feature to try and fill the remaining two days. Waitlists are a little bit tricky, so they'll have to be careful about how they do it. They could create a single waitlist to pick up both days; however, waitlists are filled in the order they were created, and so if they make one waitlist for both days, both of those days would need to open up at the same time for their waitlist to be filled. They would be better off creating one waitlist for each day they need, since DVC members can have two active waitlists at a time. Once a waitlist is filled, another one can be created.

So the Parrs could make two waitlists for Saratoga Springs, two waitlists for Animal Kingdom Lodge, or one for each. They decide to make one for each—they waitlist one day at Saratoga, adjacent to Saratoga Springs stay they already have booked, and likewise for Animal Kingdom Lodge. After one week, they find out that their Animal Kingdom Lodge waitlist came through. They call member services and have them combine the two-night reservation they already had at Animal Kingdom Lodge with the one-night reservation that was just made via their waitlist, giving them one three-night reservation at Animal Kingdom Lodge.

Remember that they also had a three-night stay reserved at Saratoga Springs at the beginning of their trip, so they only need that pesky one night in the middle that they have waitlisted at Saratoga Springs. While DVC members can only have two waitlists at a time, there are not any rules about waitlisting the same day for two different resorts, so they hedge their bets and waitlist the same day at Animal Kingdom Lodge. Luckily, after a couple of weeks their Saratoga Springs waitlist comes through, giving them a full seven-night stay—four nights at Saratoga Springs followed by three nights at Animal Kingdom Lodge Kidani.

Now all the Parrs have to do to move resorts is notify Bell Services the night before they check out at Saratoga Springs to pick up their bags in the morning and move them to Animal Kingdom Lodge Kidani.

They can then hop on a Disney bus and enjoy the parks for the day, and return to their new resort at the end of the day where their bags will already be waiting for them—Disney magic at its finest!

Even though the Parrs were trying to book a trip really late in the game, they were still able to make it work by using waitlists and a split stay.

When you make a waitlist there are some options that you need to be aware of.

First, you can choose whether or not you want the waitlist to replace an existing reservation if that waitlist comes through. For example, let's say you really wanted Animal Kingdom Lodge, but it wasn't available for the night you wanted, and Saratoga Springs *was* available. You can book Saratoga and create a waitlist for Animal Kingdom Lodge, specifying that when the AKL waitlist comes through it will replace your existing Saratoga Springs reservation.

Second, you can indicate whether or not it is okay for Disney to borrow vacation points if your waitlist comes through. If you don't choose this option, and you don't have enough points to book the waitlist in your current use year, the waitlist will not be fulfilled.

Finally, be aware that Disney will automatically cancel your waitlist 31 days before check-in date. The reason for this is a little complicated, but let's walk through it. There is no penalty for cancelling a DVC reservation 31 days or more before check in; your points simply go right back into your DVC account. Cancelling less than 31 days creates complications by placing your points in a "holding" status, which puts strict limitations on how you can use them. We'll talk in more detail shortly about "points in holding"; for now, you just need to know that while there is an option to override the 31 day automatic cancellation on waitlists, I don't recommend you choose it.

Disney trips require more planning than ever before, especially with the advent of FastPasses and advanced dining reservations. Late trip planning limits your options—it affects your room, your dining reservations, and your FastPass selections. Whether staying in a DVC resort, or any Disney resort, planning is essential to a relaxing and worry-free trip. If you plan accordingly and manage your expectations, I guarantee that your Disney trip will be magical.

Check out the "Tips and Tricks" chapter for some more great wait-list strategies and split stay ideas.

We've talked about the term "use year" in previous chapters. To refresh your memory, use year refers to the month in which you receive your points. As DVC owners, it's crucial that you are aware of the various rules and key dates involving use years. If you have an October use year you will receive you're annual allotment of points on October 1 each year, and those points will expire on September 30 of the following year if you don't use them. If you don't plan to use all of your points, you will want to bank them to the following use year, but you don't have all year to do this—points must be banked no later than eight months after your use year. So, if you have an October use year, you need to bank unused 2015 points by the end of May 2016.

The chart below shows banking deadlines for each use year:

Use Year	Last Day to Bank Points
February	September 30
March	October 31
April	November 30
June	January 31
August	March 31
September	April 30
October	May 31
December	July 31

While banking and borrowing are great features of owning DVC, you do have to be careful with them. Once points are banked, it is a final transaction. You can't return banked points to the original use year if you change your mind. Borrowing is also a final transaction. If you borrow points from the next use year to book a trip, and then need to cancel your trip, the borrowed points stay with your current use year; you can't bank them back to their original use year.

As we discussed earlier with waitlists, another term you should be aware of as a DVC owner is "points in holding". Cancelling a DVC trip more than 31 days prior to check in is not a problem—your points will be placed back into your account and you can book another trip right away. However, cancelling a DVC trip less than 31 days prior to check in will put the points from the cancelled trip into a holding status. Points in holding have strict penalties associated with them. While the points are still your property, they are not as flexible anymore. Points in holding must be used by the end of your current use year, meaning that you cannot bank these points to your next use year as you would normally be able to do. Furthermore, these points can only be used to book accommodations on 60-days' notice or less. DVC resorts are always in demand, so finding a reservation at 60 days or less before check in is not going to be easy. You're going to have to target one of the larger DVC resorts like Saratoga Springs, Old Key West, or savannah view rooms at Animal Kingdom Lodge—and you're likely going to have to be open to split stays.

Let's look at a practical example of this as it relates to Bob and Helen Parr's DVC contract. Remember that their resale contract is 150 points at Saratoga Springs, with a September use year:

> The Parrs have a magical trip planned for their family. They are planning to stay at a deluxe studio at Disney's Polynesian Resort for eight nights with a check-in date of October 23. They planned this trip early and were able to snag a reservation at the Polynesian at seven months out even though it is not their home resort. On September 30, Bob learns that his company is sending him on a mandatory business conference, so the Parrs have to cancel their trip.

> Unfortunately, now that it's the end of September, they have less than 31 days before their trip, so the 150 points they used to book this trip (all of their points for this use year) are placed into a holding status. Bob and Helen's first instinct is to bank these points to the next use year and try to book the same trip for next year; however, they can't bank them because they are in holding. They have to use their points before their use year ends on August 31 of the next year, so they decide they will try for another trip with a June 15 check-in—right after the kids get out of school.

> They go to make this reservation seven months out on November 15, but realize they are not able to do it because they must book 60 days or less prior to their check in—the result of their points being in a holding status. So, they must wait until April to book, at which time there may be little or no availability.

As you can see from this example, points that are in a holding status really tie your hands in terms of how you can use them. Unfortunately, it is a reality that sometimes you may have a situation like this to deal with, so it's important to be aware of it before buying into DVC if you think it may be an issue for you.

Now, onto a brighter aspect of the Disney Vacation Club—one that again highlights its flexibility.

Let's assume that you are booking a trip and are short by a few points, either because you don't want to borrow from the next use year or you have already borrowed all of your points. There is another alternative that Disney offers: "one-time-use" vacation points. You can obtain a maximum of 24 extra points per use year from Disney at a rate of $15 per point, including tax (as I write this).

Let's look at an example of how Bob and Helen Parr could take advantage of one-time-use points:

> *The Parrs want to get away for a quick three-night trip to celebrate their anniversary. Grandma and Grandpa Parr have offered to watch the kids, so this will be a rare adults-only trip for Bob and Helen. They plan to stay in a deluxe studio at Disney's Grand Floridian in September. They figure out that they will need 51 vacation points to book this trip; however, they only have 45 points left. They really don't want to borrow six points from the next use year, so they call up member services and purchase six extra one-time-use vacation points. At $15 per point, the total cost for their points purchase comes out to $90. Now, Bob and Helen can book their anniversary trip without having to borrow any points.*

Now for the fine print. There are several rules pertaining to one-time-use points that you need to be aware of. One-time-use points can be processed in multiple transactions, but cannot exceed 24 points in one year when combined. These points expire according to the use year for the reservation booked, are non-transferable and non-refundable, and cannot be banked or borrowed. These points also cannot be used for waitlist reservations and cannot be applied retroactively. Members must be in good standing (meaning that maintenance fees are paid up) in order to obtain these points. When booking DVC resorts, one-time-use points can be used up to seven months prior to arrival, so you won't be able to use them if you are booking your home resort eleven months prior to check in. These points are only available for DVC, Disney Collection, and World Collection resorts.

Disney Vacation Club members can use their points to book trips for other folks. This can be a great gift for family members or friends, especially if they have never been to Walt Disney World or don't have the financial means to afford a Disney trip. It can also be a great way to celebrate a special occasion for friends or loved ones.

Let's look at how Bob and Helen can use their DVC membership to gift a Walt Disney World vacation:

> *Bob Parr has always appreciated all that his parents have done for him over the years. Bob's parents have wanted to go to Walt Disney World, but were never able to afford a trip of their own. Now, Grandma and Grandpa Parr are about to celebrate their 50th wedding anniversary, and Bob and Helen really want to give them a memorable anniversary, but Bob and Helen are raising three kids of their own and they just don't have the cash to book them into a regular Disney resort.*

> *Instead, they book a trip for the grandparents using their Disney Vacation Club points. They simply go onto the DVC member website and book a trip just like they normally would, except that they put in Grandma and Grandpa Parr's names as the guests and check the box stating that they are not DVC members. Now Bob's parents can enjoy their first magical Disney trip, and Bob and Helen didn't have to pay cash to book it.*

As a DVC member, you can even rent out your points if, for one reason or another, you aren't able to use your points or if you have extra points that are about to expire. You can try to rent the points out yourself, or use an intermediary service such as DVCRequest.com.

The typical rate for renting your points out through an intermediary service fluctuates based on demand; currently, the rate is about $11—13 per point depending on your home resort, when your points expire, and the number of points you are renting. The way the intermediary service works is you first enter into an agreement with them, then they place your points in a queue. As the intermediary service receives rental requests, they contact DVC member services to check availability. Once availability is confirmed, the service polls several DVC members in the queue who are determined to be matches to see who is available to make the reservation. If you are the first to respond, the intermediary service will send you the reservation request so that you can make the reservation for the renter and provide a confirmation number to the intermediary service. They then collect the funds and immediately transfer 70% of these funds to you via PayPal. Upon the renter's check in, you receive the remaining 30% balance. They hold back 30% to ensure that you keep your maintenance fees and loan payments (if you financed your DVC membership) up to date so that reservations will not be canceled by Disney. Once the renter makes the reservation it is a non-refundable transaction, so you will receive your money no matter what.

Let's look at how Bob and Helen Parr can use this feature of the DVC account:

> Bob and Helen Parr don't anticipate taking a vacation next year, and they could really use some extra money since their daughter Violet is getting married in a few months. They decide to rent out next year's DVC points using an intermediary service like DVCRequest.com. Bob contacts the service and gives them the details of their contract: 150 points at Disney's Saratoga Springs with a September use year. The service drafts an agreement and sends it to Bob and Helen, who then sign and return the agreement. A few weeks pass by and the intermediary service matches a contract with a couple from Texas who wants to book a Christmas stay at Saratoga Springs for the following year. The trip will cost 142 points and is ten months away, but since Saratoga Springs is Bob and Helen's home resort, they can make a reservation there up to eleven months in advance.
>
> Bob and Helen make the reservation in the renter's name and send the reservation confirmation to the intermediary service. The rental agreement states that they will receive $11.30/point for the rental and a 70% payout upon completion of the reservation, so right away they receive $1,123.22. Bob and Helen make sure they stay current on their maintenance fees between now and then (they don't have loan payments to worry about because they paid cash for their DVC contract). Christmas comes the next year, the renters check in at Saratoga Springs, and the Parrs receive the remaining 30% balance: $481.38.
>
> Altogether, the Parrs make $1,604.60 by renting out their points which will help out considerably with their daughter's wedding expenses. On top of that, they still have 8 points that they can bank to the next use year,

Now, let's consider a points rental from a different perspective. Imagine for a moment that you didn't buy into the Disney Vacation Club and instead decided to rent points from an existing DVC member. As mentioned above, there are several reputable sites where you can find rentals, or you can rent directly from a DVC member with no "middleman". If you decide to rent directly from a DVC member, I want to caution you to be VERY careful—unfortunately, there have been many instances of fraud with this type of direct transaction.

There are a few scenarios that you might want to think about. First, it's possible for an owner to take your money and then cancel the reservation, and you would have no way of knowing this for sure until the moment you try to check in. A second scenario is that DVC members need to be up to date on their yearly maintenance fees and their loan payments if they financed their DVC purchase, so it's also possible that while the owner did not intentionally take your money and cancel your reservation, the reservation may have been rendered invalid by Disney because the owner is behind on payments.

With a direct transaction it is possible that you could lose all of your money, but there are some ways to reduce that likelihood. Make sure you get the owner's full name, address, and phone number prior to sending them any money. Obtain references from the owner, and make sure to follow-up and contact those references. I also suggest you talk over the phone with the owner as well; don't try to do the transaction entirely through email—if the owner doesn't want to talk over the phone, that should be a huge red flag for you. Once you have their name, address and phone number, perform a Google search on them to see if any red flags pop up; maybe someone else has been burned by them before. You can also visit the Florida Comptroller's Website, www.occompt.com (if they own a DVC resort at Walt Disney World) to confirm that person is, in fact, a DVC member. There are similar websites for Vero Beach (ori.indian-river.org), Hilton Head (rodweb.bcgov.net), and the Grand Californian (cr.ocgov.com). There is not currently an online public record for Aulani.

Only use a credit card for payments so that you have fraud protection. If the owner doesn't directly accept credit cards, you can use your credit card to pay them through PayPal. NEVER use cash, personal check, cashier's check, money orders, or "cash equivalents" like Western Union. Make sure you have a written contract with the owner clearly stating what the rental will cost, the dates of your stay, and when payments are due—this must be signed by both parties. Always make sure you receive a Disney reservation confirmation from the owner. Disney will not speak with renters or give them any information, but you can usually verify the reservation on the Disney reservations page: mydisneyreservation.com/dvc. And finally, when renting DVC points, use the gut check—if your gut tells you that something is off, DON'T PROCEED!

I think renting is a great way to get your feet wet with DVC before you buy in, but I would encourage you to avoid renting directly from owners whenever possible, even if it costs a little bit more to go through an intermediary.

Let's take a look at what could happen when a DVC points rental goes wrong:

> *Imagine for a moment that our "super couple" Bob and Helen Parr are not yet DVC owners, but they are interested in DVC. Prior to buying in they decide to try out a DVC rental to see how they like the resort and room style. They would like a standard-view deluxe studio villa at Disney's Polynesian Village for an October stay, which will require 130 vacation points. They visit a reputable DVC rental intermediary site, such as DVCRequest.com, and find that the standard cost for a point rental is $14/point (this is the cost for the renter; it's more than the price the DVC owner that is renting out the points would receive because the intermediary service needs to make their money, too). There is a $2/point upcharge for premium DVC resorts that are booked more than seven months in advance (premium resorts include Bay Lake Tower, Beach Club, Boardwalk, Wilderness Lodge, Grand Floridian, Grand Californian, Aulani, and Polynesian).*

> *The Parrs are booking less than seven months before check-in so their actual cost is still $14/point. Since they need 130 points to book this reservation, their cost would be $1820. A non-DVC reservation for a standard room at the Polynesian would likely cost the Parrs over $2500, so it seems like a good deal. However, Bob finds a DVC owner on Craigslist that is selling their points for $12/point, which would save them another $160 over using the intermediary rental site. The Parrs decide to go with the individual owner and save the money.*

> *Bob and Helen don't do any research on this owner, and all of their communication is through email, so they never actually speak with him. While the owner did book the trip for Bob and Helen as promised,*

and sent them the reservation confirmation, between the time of the rental and the Parr's check-in date the DVC owner falls behind on his maintenance fee and loan payments, unbeknownst to Bob and Helen.

October rolls around and the Parrs drive 1000 miles to Florida for their trip. They go to check in and are told the reservation was cancelled because the DVC owner fell behind on his payments. The Parrs are devastated—they've lost the money that they paid for their trip and have no accommodations. Now their only options are to lay out more money to reserve another hotel, if there are any available, or turn around and go home.

Saving that extra $160 by renting directly from the owner cost the Parrs much more in the long run—better safe than sorry!

While not every DVC rental will turn out this way, unfortunately there are more and more instances of things like this happening, even within the DVC community, so it's important to make wise, informed decisions and make sure you do the necessary research when booking through a DVC points rental.

Another great feature available to DVC members is a points transfer. This feature allows member-to-member transfer amongst Disney Vacation Club members. It's similar to renting, although it requires that both parties are DVC members. A transfer could be a rental where one DVC member has points to sell and the other needs extra points; however, I do want to caution you that this is against official Disney Vacation Club rules which state that a point transfer cannot be for financial gain. More likely, a points transfer will be gifted between friends or family.

Whatever the reason for the transfer, there are rules that you should be aware of. You are limited to one transfer per membership, per use year (not calendar year). This rule applies for transfers into, and out of, your account. So, if you've already transferred points to somebody else, you cannot receive a transfer, and vice versa. Additionally, points that are transferred maintain their home resort and use year, even if the receiving member has a different resort and/or use year. All transfers are final transactions and cannot be reversed, and banked/borrowed points cannot be transferred, although the receiving member can bank the points once they're in his account. Both the transferring and receiving members must be current on their maintenance fees and loan payments. Lastly, the transferring member is still responsible for paying maintenance fees on the transferred points; this responsibility does not transfer to the receiving member.

Let's look at how the Parrs can use the points transfer feature:

> *Bob and Helen have some extra points this year that they don't plan on using. They were going to bank them, but they found out that Bob's sister Ashleigh, a fellow DVC member, needs some extra points for a trip she is planning. Bob and Helen decide to help her out and gift some of their extra points to Ashleigh so that she can book her trip. They call up member services to complete the transaction. In order to do this, they will need both membership numbers and the number of points to be transferred. While they initiate the transfer over the phone, the transfer will need to be confirmed in writing by mail, fax, or email. Ashleigh is elated to receive these points and can now book her trip.*

We've covered quite a bit of ground in this chapter, but there are so many ins and outs to the Disney Vacation Club that it's important you fully understand how the program works before you buy into it, and certainly before you start using it. By knowing the rules pertaining to each aspect of DVC, you will not be caught in a sticky situation where you aren't able to maximize the use of your points.

As we move on from the details of using DVC, we now come to a chapter that you will find interesting and enlightening: DVC discounts and perks!

SIX

DVC Discounts and Perks

When you buy into the Disney Vacation Club, you will unlock many savings opportunities and exclusive member experiences—there are almost too many to count! When I first joined DVC, I felt like I had a pretty good handle on all of the discounts that were now available to me. However, I soon found out on our first DVC trip that there were quite a few I didn't even know about.

Earlier in this book, we looked at a financial analysis of a direct-from-Disney DVC purchase and a resale purchase. We didn't take into account all of the discounts that DVC members can enjoy. If you're not yet convinced of what a great value DVC really is, you might be after reading this chapter!

The major expenses of any Disney trip are lodging, tickets, food, and souvenirs. Just by buying into the Disney Vacation club, you've already taken care of the lodging part—from now on you will book your trips using DVC points instead of cash. But what about the other expenses? Let's take a look at each of them to see how DVC will save you money.

We'll start with my personal favorite: tickets. Disney Vacation Club members and their immediate family living in the same household currently receive discounts on both annual passes and premier annual passes. An annual pass gives you unlimited admission for 365 days to all four of Walt Disney World's theme parks and allows for unlimited park hopping. It does not, however, include waterpark admission. A premium annual pass gives you access to the four theme parks plus Disney's Typhoon Lagoon and Blizzard Beach water parks, Disney's Oak Trail Golf Course, and ESPN Wide World of Sports. Annual pass-holders enjoy many discounts as well, some of which are the save as a DVC member would get, and some that are exclusive to the annual passholder program, so being a DVC member *with* an annual pass maximizes the number of discounts you are eligible for.

Here's a breakdown of the annual pass and premier annual pass prices:

Annual Pass (2015, includes tax):

- First Year: $563.39
- Renewals: $478.19

Premier Annual Pass (2015, includes tax):

- First Year: $691.19
- Renewal: $584.69

You can purchase the passes online, by telephone, or in person at Walt Disney World. Renewals can be made 60 days prior to, or up to 30 days after, the expiration of your existing annual pass. If you purchase your tickets online or over the phone, you will receive a voucher number you can use to link your pass to your MyDisneyExperience (MDE) online account, after which you'll just need your MagicBand for park admission. You will also need to stop by will-call either at Disney Springs or one of the parks to pick up the physical ticket. You don't need the physical ticket to get into the parks if your pass is properly linked to your MDE account, but you will need your annual passholder card to get your AP discounts, just like you need your DVC membership card to get your DVC discounts. Unfortunately cast members cannot (at present) use your MagicBand to give you your discount (even if you have those cool little DVC and/or annual passholder sliders for your MagicBand).

The DVC annual pass discount is a great feature of DVC, but you shouldn't necessarily base your decision on buying into DVC solely on receiving this discount because all DVC discounts are subject to change—there is nothing in your DVC contract that entitles you to discounted tickets; it is merely a perk that Disney chooses to offer. There have been some rumors in recent years that this discount could go away, but it's here right now, so why not use it! Disney also periodically offers discounts on other tickets such as four- or five-day tickets. Limited time discounts like these will be listed on the DVC website, so it's always good to check there every so often for new or limited-time discounts.

If you opt to get a regular annual pass, you will still receive a discount on water park tickets. The DVC discount for Disney's water parks is $4 per one-day adult ticket and $3 per one-day child ticket, and is valid both at Typhoon Lagoon and Blizzard Beach. If you're not afraid of heights, you may want to try the Aerophile Hot-Air Balloon ride at Disney Springs, which offers a discounted rate of $10 for both adult and child tickets between the hours of 8:30am and 10:30am. Hot-air balloon rides after 10:30am are discounted by 20% for DVC members.

If behind the scenes tours of the theme parks interest you, DVC members are eligible for a 15% discount. This is an activity that I had never experienced until becoming a member, and I recommend it. We tried a backstage tour on our second DVC trip and now try to go on a new tour each time we visit. I was aware of these tours prior to joining DVC, but never really considered taking one because of the cost. Now, with my DVC discount, it makes sense. Many of these tours take you behind the scenes at Disney's theme parks to see how the magic works. On longer tours, lunch is often included in the price of the tour, so it ends up being a pretty good deal. I recommend trying the Keys to the Kingdom tour at the Magic Kingdom. It is a 4–5 hour tour that takes you behind the scenes of the Magic Kingdom to show how the amazing cast members at Walt Disney World make our vacations so magical. Lunch at the Columbia Harbour House is included. This is probably the most well-known and popular tour because it takes you down into the infamous "utilidors" beneath the Magic Kingdom to see how cast members can travel through the park without being seen. Another cool feature about this tour (and many others) is admission into the park before it actually opens, making for some really great photo opportunities.

Another big part of your vacation expense will be food. Disney has some great restaurants, and as a DVC member you're going to be able to save money at many of them. Many folks who aren't Disney regulars have a perception that Disney food is just all fast food—hamburgers, chicken nuggets, and fries. But we know that this is not the case at all. Walt Disney World has probably the widest variety of restaurants that you could find in one place. They have everything from counter service for those in a hurry, to table service for those looking for a traditional sit-down meal, to dinner shows featuring entertainment and great food, and even five-star restaurants for those with a more generous vacation budget. The cuisine is not just limited to American food, either; there are cuisines from around the globe, especially in World Showcase at Epcot. Whatever your taste or dining style preference, DVC offers plenty of discounts to its members.

Sometimes it can be difficult to figure out which restaurants offer DVC discounts, and how much of a discount, so I'm going to walk you through each dining discount. I do warn you, however, that these discounts are subject to change, and it's always best to double check with a Disney cast member.

You'll find some of the best dining options at Epcot, especially around World Showcase, where you can find much global cuisine. If you visit in the fall during Epcot's International Food & Wine Festival, you'll have even more choices. DVC members receive the following discounts at Epcot:

10% off food at:

- Biergarten in Germany
- San Angel Inn in Mexico
- La Hacienda de San Angel in Mexico
- Nine Dragons in China
- Teppan Edo in Japan

15% off food at:

- Chefs de France in France
- Via Napoli in Italy
- Tutto Italia in Italy

20% off food at:

- Restaurant Marrekesh in Morocco
- Tokyo Dining in Japan

While Epcot is the park to be in for food, the other parks have some really great and unique dining options as well. If you're visiting the Animal Kingdom, you can receive 10% off your meal at the Rainforest Café as well as at Yak & Yeti. Hollywood Studios discounts include 10% off at both the Hollywood Brown Derby and Hollywood & Vine. Unfortunately, there are no dining discount at the Magic Kingdom for DVC members or annual passholders, but there is another discount called the Tables in Wonderland card that is available to DVC members and Florida residents. We'll talk about that shortly.

Disney Springs offers great dining, shopping, and entertainment, and is a must-do for our family on each trip. This area, formerly known as Downtown Disney, is currently undergoing a major refurbishment and re-theming that will bring about some incredible new dining and shopping opportunities. There are some really great dining discounts at Disney Springs:

10% off food at:

- Earl of Sandwich
- Cookies of Dublin
- Fulton's Crab House
- Ghirardelli
- Hill of Beans
- House of Blues
- Planet Hollywood
- Portobello
- Raglan Road
- Rainforest Café
- T-Rex
- Wolfgang Puck Café

20% off food at:

- Haagan-Dazs
- Paradiso 37
- Bodie's All-American
- Wetzel's Pretzels

This may be surprising to some, but I think many of the best dining locations at Walt Disney World can be found at the Disney resorts. There are plenty of DVC dining discounts to be had at each resort, no matter your taste. As a DVC member you are eligible for 10% off of your food purchase at the following resort dining locations:

Disney's Animal Kingdom Resort:

- Sanaa (Kidani Village)
- Boma (Jambo House)

Disney's Boardwalk Inn:

- Big River Grille and Brewing Works

ESPN Club

- Flying Fish Café
- Trattoria al Forno

Disney's Contemporary Resort:

- The Wave...of American Flavors

Disney's Fort Wilderness Resort & Campground

- Trail's End
- Disney's Wilderness Lodge Resort
- Whispering Canyon Café
- Artist Point

Disney's Grand Floridian Resort & Spa

- Grand Floridian Café
- Citrico's

Disney's Old Key West Resort

- Olivia's Café

Disney's Saratoga Springs Resort & Spa

- Turf Club Bar & Grill

Disney's Yacht Club Resort

- Captain's Grill

As I teased earlier in this chapter, there are even better dining discounts available to DVC members through a discount program known as Tables in Wonderland. This little-known treasure can save you quite a bit on dining, especially if you tend toward table-service restaurants. The Tables in Wonderland discount card is available only to DVC members, annual passholders, and Florida residents. It gives you a 20% discount on most table-service restaurants in Disney World, as well as lounges and even a few counter-service locations. The unique aspect to this discount card, that you won't find with too many discount programs, is that it includes both food and alcohol!

Here's a list of Tables in Wonderland restaurants at Disney World:

Magic Kingdom:
- Be Our Guest (Fantasyland, dinner only)
- Cinderella's Royal Table (Fantasyland)
- Liberty Tree Tavern (Liberty Square)
- The Crystal Palace (Main Street, USA)
- The Plaza Restaurant (Main Street, USA)
- Tony's Town Square Restaurant (Main Street, USA)

Epcot:
- Akershus Royal Banquet Hall (Norway)
- Biergarten Restaurant (Germany)
- Coral Reef Restaurant (Future World—The Seas)
- Le Cellier Steakhouse (Canada)
- Les Chefs de France (France, lunch only)
- Nine Dragons Restaurant (China)
- Restaurant Marrakesh (Morocco)
- Rose & Crown Pub & Dining Room (United Kingdom)
- San Angel Inn Restaurante (Mexico)
- Spice Road Table (Morocco)
- The Garden Grill Restaurant (Future World—The Land)
- Tokyo Dining (Japan)
- Tutto Italia Ristorante (Italy)
- Via Napoli Ristorante e Pizzeria (Italy)

Hollywood Studios:
- 50's Prime Time Café
- Hollywood & Vine
- Mama Melrose's Ristorante Italiano
- Sci-Fi Dine-in Theater
- The Hollywood Brown Derby
- Tune-In Lounge

Animal Kingdom:
- Flame Tree Barbecue

- Pizzafari
- Restaurantosaurus
- Tusker House Restaurant

Disney Springs:

- Fulton's Crab House
- House of Blues (excludes Sunday Brunch)
- Paradiso 37, Taste of the Americas
- Planet Hollywood
- Portobello
- Raglan Road Irish Pub and Restaurant
- Splitsville (excludes merchandise and bowling)
- Wolfgang Puck Café

ESPN Wide World of Sports:

- ESPN's Wide World of Sports Grill

Disney's All-Star Movies Resort:

- World Premiere Food Court (counter service)

Disney's All-Star Music Resort:

- Intermission Food Court (counter service)

Disney's All-Star Sports Resort:

- End Zone Food Court (counter service)

Disney's Animal Kingdom Lodge, Jambo House:

- Boma—Flavors of Africa
- Cape Town Lounge and Wine Bar
- Jiko—The Cooking Place
- Victoria Falls

Disney's Animal Kingdom Lodge, Kidani Village:

- Sanaa

Disney's Art of Animation Resort:

- Landscape of Flavors (counter service)

Disney's Beach Club Resort:
- Beaches & Cream Soda Shop (excludes take-out)
- Ca[e May Café
- Martha's Vineyard Lounge

Disney's Boardwalk Resort:
- Belle Vue Lounge (excludes breakfast)
- Big River Grille & Brewing Works
- ESPN Club
- Flying Fish Café
- Trattoria al Forno

Disney's Caribbean Beach Resort:
- Shutters at Old Pointe Royale

Disney's Contemporary Resort:
- California Grill
- Chef Mickey's
- Outer Rim
- The Wave...of American Flavors

Disney's Coronado Springs Resort:
- Maya Grill

Disney's Fort Wilderness Resort & Campground:
- Crockett's Tavern
- Hoop-Dee-Doo Musical Revue (late show only)
- Trail's End Restaurant (excludes take-out)
- Mickey's Backyard BBQ

Disney's Grand Floridian Resort & Spa:
- 1900 Park Fare
- Citricos
- Grand Floridian Café
- Mizner's Lounge
- Narcoossee's

Disney's Old Key West Resort:

- Olivia's Café
- Gurgling Suitcase

Disney's Polynesian Resort:

- 'Ohana
- Kona Café
- Spirit of Aloha Dinner Show (late show only)
- Tambu Lounge

Disney's Pop Century Resort:

- Everything Pop Shopping & Dining (counter service, excludes merchandise)

Disney's Port Orleans Resort—French Quarter:

- Sassagoula Floatworks and Food Factory (counter service)
- Scat Cat's Club

Disney's Port Orleans Resort—Riverside:

- Boatwright's Dining Hall
- River Roost

Disney's Saratoga Springs Resort & Spa:

- The Artist's Palette (counter service)
- The Turf Club Bar and Grill
- The Turf Club Lounge

Disney's Vero Beach Resort:

- The Green Cabin Room
- Shutters
- Sonya's

Disney's Wilderness Lodge:

- Artist Point
- Territory Lounge
- Whispering Canyon Café

Walt Disney World Swan & Dolphin Resorts:

- Garden Grove

- Il Mulino New York Trattoria
- Kimonas
- Shula's Steak House
- Todd English's bluezoo

Disney's Yacht Club Resort:

- Ale and Compass Lounge
- Captain's Grille
- Crew's Cub Lounge
- Yachtsman Steakhouse

The Tables in Wonderland discount card does have some blackout dates. It's not valid on holidays (Mother's Day, Easter Sunday, Independence Day, Thanksgiving Day, Christmas Eve, Christmas Day, New Year's Eve, and New Year's Day). Additionally, some restaurants have longer blackout periods. These restaurants include 1900 Park Fare, Chef Mickey's, 'Ohana (dinner only), Cinderella's Royal Table, LeChefs de France, Akershus Royal Banquet Hall, and Le Cellier steakhouse. Typically, these periods fall during the spring break season, Memorial Day through most of June, Thanksgiving week, and Christmas week. Also be aware that an 18% gratuity will be automatically added to your bill when you use your Tables in Wonderland card.

The Tables in Wonderland card is currently $100 for DVC members and annual passholders, and $125 for Florida residents. The card is good for 13 months, which means if you visit Walt Disney World around the same time every year, there's a good chance you can get two trips in on one discount card. One card gives you a discount for up to 10 adults as long as they are all on one bill (no check-splitting). You do have the option of buying an extra card for $50, but since one card covers 10 adults, most folks find it's not necessary to purchase one. Unfortunately, you can't buy the Tables in Wonderland card online; you must visit a guest relations location at a Walt Disney World theme park or at Disney Springs, bringing with you both a photo ID and your DVC membership card. The TIW card is physical media and there is a $50 replacement fee if something happens to it, so you may want to put it in a plastic Ziploc bag before taking it onto Splash Mountain or Kali River Rapids. If you are a DVC member who likes table-service dining, don't leave home without this card!

Another vacation expense that can be large depending on your habits is souvenirs. Disney has a lot of great merchandise and keepsakes to take home with you. There are a lot of great shopping locations at the resorts, parks, and at Disney Springs. This is one expense that I always tend to under-budget for, no matter how hard we try to keep our souvenir expenses down. Plus, if you're a DVC member you need to get some bling to show that you *are* a member! Thankfully, members can save money on all of that great Disney merchandise. All Disney-owned-and-operated merchandise locations offer a 10% discount to DVC members. There are even some non-Disney owned establishments at Walt Disney World that offer discounts to members, such as a 10% discount at all Sunglass Hut locations and several Disney Springs shops and stores (Arribas Brothers, Curl by Sammy Duvall, House of Blues Company Store, the Pearl Factory, the Planet Hollywood store, Pop Gallery, and RideMakers). A 15% discount is available at select locations such as the Rainforest Café Retail Villages at Animal Kingdom and Disney Springs, as well as Yak and Yeti at Animal Kingdom, and Basin, LittleMissMatched, and T-Rex Café's Dino Store at Disney Springs. Members can even save 20% on Disney family portraits.

I find that there are so many discount with DVC it's often hard to remember them all and keep them straight. The best way to make sure you receive all of your discounts is to ask a cast member if there is a DVC discount (or an annual passholder discount if you are also one of those) whenever you're paying for something at Walt Disney World—if they don't know for sure, they will ask their manager.

This has been a pretty long list of discounts, but believe it or not, we're not done yet! One aspect of staying at a DVC resort is that they are equipped with DVD players. This is great, but if you didn't happen to bring any of your own DVDs, you're out of luck, right? Wrong! Disney offers free DVD rentals to DVC members at most DVC resorts. So, if it's a rainy day, or maybe you just want to kick back in your room and watch a movie, don't forget about this unique DVC perk.

As a DVC member you will also receive a discount at several Children's Activity Centers at Walt Disney World. We all love our kids, but sometimes it's nice to have a little one-on-one time with your spouse for a nice dinner, shopping, or even visiting the theme parks. We sometimes travel with my in-laws and they offer to watch the kids so that my wife and I can have a date night while we're on vacation. This is nice, but not everyone has extended family to travel with. The children's activity centers at Disney resorts are a great way for both kids and adults to have fun. DVC members will receive a 15% discount at the Cub's Den at Disney's Wilderness Lodge, Lilo's Playhouse at Disney's Polynesian Resort, the Sandcastle Club at Disney's Yacht & Beach Club resorts, and Simba's Cubhouse at Disney's Animal Kingdom Lodge. Hours of operation at these children's centers are 4:30pm to midnight. Children ages 3–12 are welcome, and the discount is limited to three children per member. Children must be potty-trained, and a minimum of 2 hours will be charged. The clubs are very safe and are comparable to the children's areas on the Disney cruise ships. I can tell you from experience that your kids will have so much fun here that they won't want you to pick them up!

There's a plethora of recreation to enjoy at Walt Disney World, even without stepping foot into a theme park or water park, and most of these recreation experiences are discounted for DVC members. You and up to three of your non-DVC member guests can enjoy a 35% discount at Disney's Palm Golf Course, Magnolia Golf Course, and Lake Buena Vista Golf Course. The discount is valid from the first tee time each morning until twilight rates begin. Junior golfers 17 and under can play at 50% off the regular rate. Disney's Oak Trail 9-hole Walking Golf Course is only $20 per round for DVC members. DVC members can also receive 20% off on golf lessons. These 45-minute long lessons are taught by PGA instructors and are customized to your skill and experience level. Walt Disney World also has two themed miniature golf locations: Disney's Winter Summerland Miniature Golf Course (located near Blizzard Beach) and Fantasia Garden's Miniature Golf Course (located near the Swan & Dolphin). Tennis lessons are also available at a discounted rate of 10% off the regular price. These hour-long lessons are taught by USPTA certified professionals and are customized to your skill set.

There are also several Walt Disney World resorts that offer marina rentals: Disney's Contemporary Resort, Fort Wilderness, Grand Floridian, Polynesian, Wilderness Lodge, Yacht Club, and Old Key West resorts. As a DVC member you will receive 15% off most rentals. This discount is available on pontoon boats, sea raycers, and canoes. Additionally, most marinas also rent bicycles and surrey bicycles—you'll receive 15% off of these (except at Disney's Boardwalk

Inn). DVC members also receive 15% off guided fishing excursions. Please note that marina rentals are first-come, first-serve, and do not accept reservations. The DVC discount is not valid on golf carts or specialty cruises.

Disney recently started offering a new type of recreation experience at Disney Springs: Amphibicar Guided Tours. Amphibicars are vintage looking cars that can travel on both land and water. The Amphibicar tour lasts about 20 minutes and DVC members receive 15% off. I have yet to try this new experience, but it sure sounds like a lot of fun.

The Tri-Circle-D Ranch at Disney's Fort Wilderness Resort and Campground is another great recreation alternative at Walt Disney World. The ranch offers 10% off select activities for DVC members. Activities include a 45-minute guided trail ride through Fort Wilderness, as well as horse-drawn carriage rides for up to four guests. The Tri-Circle-D Ranch is a great place to take kids if you want a break from the crowds at the theme parks.

If you love to be pampered, then you're going to love this next discount! DVC members enjoy 15% off spa treatments of 50 minutes or more at Senses—A Disney Spa. You can visit Senses either at the Grand Floridian or Saratoga Springs. DVC members will also receive 15% off salon and nail services over $45, or fitness center massage treatments of 50 minutes or more. The savings don't end there: you're also eligible for 10% off on all retail items at Senses Spa. Unknown to many, there is actually a third spa at Walt Disney World—Mandara Spa at the Swan and Dolphin. As a DVC member, you will receive 20% off on all services Monday through Thursday, or 10% off all services Friday through Sunday at Mandara Spa.

Disney Vacation Club members can also save on Best Friends Pet Care at Walt Disney World. Members receive an additional $2 off the already discounted resort rates for both dog and cat boarding and full-day daycare. Stays of 6 hours or less will be $1 off.

We've covered quite a few discounts in this chapter, but keep in mind that they're always changing, so check the Disney Vacation Club website to get the latest and greatest information. On top of the numerous discounts we just explored, there are many exclusive member experiences that only Disney Vacation Club members can enjoy. One such experience is weekly member mixers, typically held every Wednesday at the Atlantic Dance Hall at Disney's Boardwalk Inn. These mixers are free to DVC members and feature free refreshments and free DVC merchandise that you can't buy anywhere. The mixers offer the unique opportunity to meet other DVC members or speak with DVC associates who can answer any DVC questions you might have. Another great member exclusive is access to the Top-of-the-World Lounge at Bay Lake Tower. This lounge is open only to DVC members staying at Walt Disney World using their DVC points, so if you have guests that are staying there on your points, they will not be able to access this lounge. It's one of the best places to view the Magic Kingdom fireworks. The lounge features drinks as well as a limited snack menu.

Each year Disney also offers exclusive Disney Vacation Club cruises. These cruises are a great way to connect with other DVC members while enjoying the spectacular dining and activities that a Disney cruise offers. Disney likes to take care of its DVC members, so on your DVC member cruise you will receive exclusive gifts that are available nowhere else. You don't have to use your points to book one of these cruises (remember that earlier we talked about how it is more cost-efficient to pay for a Disney cruise as opposed to using your points for booking), but you must have bought your DVC contract through Disney—unfortunately, those of us who bought resale contracts cannot experience these cruises.

There is one more unique perk for DVC members at Walt Disney World: pool hopping! I think most DVC members aren't even aware that this is allowed. What is pool hopping? It's the practice of using pools at Disney resorts other than the one you are staying at. Now, I know a thing or two about pool hopping because our family used to do this on a regular basis when I was younger. We always camped at Disney's Fort Wilderness Resort & Campground when I was growing up. Fort Wilderness had a very nice pool (it's even nicer now that they've added a water slide and kids splash area), but my parents loved to explore all of the Disney resorts during our trips. Our favorite resort to visit was the Polynesian. When I was a kid you could take a bus from Fort Wilderness to the Ticket and Transportation Center and then walk over to the Polynesian. Visiting the pool at the Polynesian became a tradition for us. We would stay there all day, order some fruit or a Dole Whip, and enjoy the tranquility of the resort.

While pool hopping was somewhat common in the 80s and 90s, today Disney generally discourages it and have even added gates to some of the nicer pools around Disney property. While Disney discourages pool hopping for most guests, they do allow DVC members to pool hop. There are limitations. A few resorts restrict their pools to guests staying there: Disney's Art of Animation, the Samawati Springs and Uzima pools at Disney's Animal Kingdom Lodge, Stormalong Bay at Disney's Beach Club, the Bay Cove Pool at Bay Lake Tower, and the recently completed Nanea Volcano Pool at the Polynesian.

DVC member discounts are not just for stays at Walt Disney World. Remember that there are four DVC resorts outside of Disney World: Disney's Grand Californian at Disneyland in California, Aulani in Hawaii, Hilton Head Island in South Carolina, and Vero Beach on the Florida coast. Let's first head over to California and see what types of discounts are offered at Disneyland.

DVC members receive a 10% discount at the following dining locations in the Disneyland Park:

- Bengal Barbecue
- Big Thunder Ranch Barbecue
- Blue Bayou Restaurant
- Café Orleans
- Carnation Café
- Clarabelle's
- Daisy's Diner
- French Market Restaurant
- The Golden Horseshoe
- Jolly Holiday Bakery Café
- Harbour Galley
- Hungry Bear Restaurant
- Little Red Wagon
- Plaza Inn
- Pluto's Dog House
- Rancho del Zocale Restaurante
- Redd Rockett's Pizza Port

- Refreshment Corner
- Royal Street Veranda
- River Belle Terrace
- Stage Door Café
- Tomorrowland Terrace
- Troubadour Tavern
- Village Haus Restaurant

The list doesn't end there. At Disney's California Adventure, DVC members receive a 10% discount at the following dining locations:

- Alfresco Tasting Terrace
- Ariel's Grotto
- Award Wieners
- Boardwalk Pizza and Pasta
- Carthay Circle Restaurant and Lounge
- Cocina Cucamonga Mexican Grill
- Corn Dog Castle
- Cove Bar
- Fiddler, Fifer & Practical Café
- Flo's V8 Café
- Lucky Fortune Cookery
- Mendocino Terrace
- Pacific Wharf Café
- Paradise Garden Grill
- Sonoma Terrace
- Studio Catering Truck
- Taste Pilots' Grill
- Wine Country Trattoria

While the Disneyland Resort is nowhere near the size of Walt Disney World, it does have three resort hotels as well as a Downtown Disney shopping and dining area. Let's take a look at discounts at each of these locations.

At the Disneyland Hotel, DVC members enjoy a 10% dining discount at:

- Goofy's Kitchen
- The Lounge at Steakhouse 55
- Steakhouse 55
- Tangora Terrace Casual Island Dining
- Trader Sam's Enchanted Tiki Bar

At Disney's Grand Californian Resort & Spa, DVC members enjoy a 10% dining discount at:

- Hearthstone Lounge
- Storytellers Café
- White Water Snacks

At Disney's Paradise Pier Hotel D,VC members enjoy a 10% dining discount at:

- Disney's PCH Grill
- Surfside Lounge

And finally, at Disneyland's Downtown Disney District, DVC members receive a 15% dining discount at the House of Blues and a 10% dining discount at the following locations:

- Catal Restaurant & Uva Bar
- Earl of Sandwich Restaurant
- ESPN Zone
- Haagan-Dazs
- Jamba Juice
- La Brea Bakery & Café
- Naples Ristorante e Pizzeria
- Napolini
- Rainforest Café (breakfast and lunch before 4pm)
- Ralph Brennan's Jazz Kitchen ($40 max discount)
- Tortilla Jo's
- Taqueria at Tortilla Jo's
- Wetzel's Pretzels

Dining discounts at the Disneyland Resort are valid for parties up to 8 and cover only food and non-alcoholic beverages.

These discounts are not exclusive to dining, either. There are also several shopping discounts and freebies. Just like at Walt Disney World, you will receive a 10% discount at all Disney-owned-and-operated merchandise locations at Disneyland when you present your DVC membership card. Another little-known perk for DVC members is at the Mlle. Antoinette's Parfumerie in New Orleans Square—you receive a complimentary hand massage and fragrance sample, as well as 10% off your fragrance purchase. Over at Disneyland's Downtown Disney District, you receive 10% off your purchase at Fossil, Quicksilver, House of Blues store, Something Silver, and Rainforest Café gift shop. At LittleMissMatched you receive 15% off on any purchase. DVC members receive a free stamped design matting on all caricatures, as well as $2.00 off any face painting. At the ESPN Zone interactive sports arena, DVC members receive double points when purchasing a new game card. At Ridemakerz DVC. members receive a free backpack with any ride purchase of $40 or more. And finally, DVC members receive 20% off on all spa services Monday-Thursday, 10% off spa services on Friday-Sunday, and 10% off retail at the Mandara Spa.

Now that we've covered all discounts at Walt Disney World and Disneyland, let's take a look at discounts at each of the other DVC resorts. At Disney's Aulani resort in Hawaii, DVC members receive 15% off on lunch dining at the Hard Rock Café between the hours of 11am and 4pm, as well as 15% off retail purchases. At the Olelo Room, DVC members receive an exclusive cocktail called the Pu'u Kilo between 5pm and 6pm daily (the cost of the cocktail is currently $7.00 plus tax and gratuity). DVC members also receive a 10% shopping discount at Disney-operated merchandise locations (Kalepa's, Hale Manu, and Lava Shack). At Laniwai—A Disney Spa, DVC members receive a complimentary upgrade on select spa treatments. At Hilo Hattie, DVC members receive a free box of chocolate-covered macadamia nuts with a $35 purchase. At Maui Divers Jewelry ,DVC members receive a free sterling silver Hawaiian Black Coral pendant and chain with any $100 purchase.

While there may not be a theme park at Aulani, there is plenty to do. The Rack A Hula Legendary Cocktail Show features "Elvis" and an all-star cast of tribute artists, hula dancers, and a live band. DVC members receive $10 off the Legendary Cocktail Show package. If a dinner cruise is more your style, DVC members receive $10 off the Star Sunset Dinner & Show package, as well as the Dolphin Star Wild Dolphin Watch and BBQ tour. There's plenty of other recreation to enjoy in and around Aulani as well. DVC members receive $10 off the exclusive golf clinic at the Ko Olina Golf Club, as well as 10% off retail items. If you love watersports, stop by the Ko Olina Marina where you receive 10% off marina boat activities. Other recreation discounts include 10% off on beach rentals, 10% off Rainbow Reef, and 10% off full-day Cabana rentals.

Disney's Hilton Head Island Resort also offers a wide variety of discounts to DVC members. New York Pizza offers a 15% discount on all food items, and several area restaurants offer a 10% discount:

- Signals (Wednesdays only)
- Tide me over (Wednesdays only)
- Frankie Bones
- San Miguels
- The Jazz Corner
- Giuseppi's Pizza & Pasta
- Old Oyster Factory
- Scott's Fish Market
- Black Marlin Bayside Grill
- A Lowcountry Backyard Restaurant
- Hugo's

Like all DVC resorts, you receive a 10% shopping discount at all Disney-owned-and-operated merchandise locations at Disney's Hilton Head Island Resort. You also receive a free coupon book for Tanger Outlet Center as well as a children's gift when you show your DVC member card at Tanger's Shopper Services. Guests ages 5–12 can enjoy $5 off on Kids' Night In, or $5 off for guests 13–17 for Teen Night In. These are three-hour-long evening programs with games and challenges, and include pizza and soda.

The final DVC resort we'll look at is Vero Beach. Here, DVC members save 10% at these dining locations:

- Shutters (breakfast and dinner only, not valid for character dining, Sunday brunch, seafood buffet, or to-go orders)

- Sonya's (breakfast discount on Saturday only, dinner discount Sunday–Thursday)

DVC members staying at Disney's Vero Beach Resort also receive $1.00 off on specialty drinks at the Green Cabin Room on Thursdays. Vero Beach offers the standard 10% off at Disney-owned-and-operated merchandise locations, as well as complimentary DVD rentals and video game rentals. There are many recreational activity discounts at Vero Beach. Members can save $2–$3 on craft experiences for kids and $5 at the Disney Discover Club, which is an evening (5–8pm) program for kids ages 4–12 that offers games, crafts, dinner, and fun. The program is offered on Mondays, Wednesdays, Fridays, and Saturdays. DVC members can visit Eb & Flo's rentals for several discounts:

- $2 off on daily beach chair rental
- $3 off on daily beach umbrella rental
- $5 off on daily cabana rental
- $7 off on daily rental of two lounge chairs and one umbrella
- $2 off on daily rental of body boards
- $10 off on one-hour rental of Hobie Cats
- $5 off on one-hour rental of kayaks
- $10 off on half-hour rental of Wave Runners
- $3 off on daily rental of bikes
- $2 off on one-hour rental of bikes
- $1 off per game of miniature golf
- Free round of miniature golf on Thursdays only
- $5 off on Fishing Fundamentals for ages 7 and older
- $5 off kayak adventures for guests ages 8 and older (guests under 18 must be accompanied by an adult)
- $5 off on Pilican Island Bike Adventure (10-mile bike ride offered seasonally, offered to all ages, but guests under 18 must be accompanied by an adult)
- $5 off on surfing lessons
- Tennis courts / racket rental for three hours is complimentary for DVC members
- $5 off on tennis lessons (30 or 60 minutes)

There is a seemingly endless list of discounts and perks at the various Disney resort locations for DVC members. Keep in mind that discounts change all of the time. I've listed the discounts available to DVC members as of the writing of this book. However, new discounts pop up every so often, certain discounts may be terminated, and the amount of the discount may change. It's always best to check the Disney Vacation Club website for the most up-to-date information. If you're on vacation and aren't sure about a discount, simply ask a cast member—they are always glad to help.

The discounts that have benefitted my family the most have been the dining discounts and, in particular, purchasing the Tables in Wonderland discount card. The annual pass discount is also a big money saver for us, and not just because of the reduced DVC price—it's also because an annual pass will open up even more savings opportunities for you. The one discount I always seem to forget about is the 10% discount on merchandise at Disney-owned-and-operated stores. There are a couple of times that I've forgotten to use it, so my advice to you is always ask if there's a DVC (or AP) discount; the worst the cast member can tell you is no.

I hope this chapter has given you a clearer picture of all the discounts available to you as a DVC member, and if you were still on the fence about buying into DVC, maybe you've now made up your mind. Next, we'll look at some insider tips to help you get the most out of your DVC membership.

SEVEN

Tips and Tricks

If I had to choose a chapter in this book that is my favorite, one that I have been looking forward to writing more than any other, it would be this one. Before buying into the Disney Vacation Club, I looked for a book that provided tips and tricks similar to what I'm about to share with you—tips not only for using the Disney Vacation Club, but also tips for buying into it. I was not able to find a book that helped in this way, so I decided to write my own. While there are a few books out there on DVC, none had everything that I wanted. I turned to the internet and found forums like MouseOwners.com and DISboards.com to help me. While these sites did help, I learned even more just by going through the process of buying my first contract, and then using it.

My purpose for writing this book was to pass this knowledge on to you with the hope that you will avoid any mistakes that I, and many others, have made in the past. I'm a firm believer that mistakes are okay as long as you learn from them, but why should you repeat the mistakes that others have already made? Even seasoned Disney Vacation Club members are not always aware of many of the tips and tricks that can help maximize DVC ownership.

I've touched on some of these tips throughout the book, so a few may seem repetitive, but I wanted to consolidate my best advice into this chapter.

Buying Resale

- When buying resale contracts, don't be afraid to negotiate the price with the seller. Just like buying a house, everything is negotiable. You can negotiate the price per point, who pays the closings costs, etc. How do you know what to offer? Visit websites like MouseOwners.com and ask questions in their forums. Often you will find others that are looking to buy a DVC contract, or some that have recently bought a contract, and they can tell you how much they are offering. There is so much that goes into the value of a DVC contract, including home resort, banked/borrowed points, and maintenance fees. No two resale contracts are the same, but you can get a pretty good idea of where to start. I recommend starting at a price point that is a little bit less than you are willing to pay. Usually, the seller will come back with a counteroffer, and if your initial offer is a little lower than you were really looking to pay, maybe the counteroffer is right on the money.

- While there is no clear-cut guide to making sure Disney doesn't exercise ROFR on your resale contract, there are some things that seem to help. Being a first-time DVC buyer helps—Disney wants more DVC members, whether it is through direct or resale purchases. More DVC members means more people in the parks, more people buying merchandise, and more people dining in Disney restaurants. Don't negotiate to have the seller pay the current year's maintenance fees. If you, as the buyer, pay the current use year's maintenance fees, it demonstrates to Disney that you are able and willing to pay these fees in the future (many DVC contracts are lost to foreclosure when people don't pay their yearly maintenance fees). Grossly undercutting the current price-per-point market can also expose you to ROFR, even if you are a first-time buyer, so make sure you research to see what most are paying and take into account whether the contract has banked points—those contracts have a higher value.

- One of the best tips for buying resale is *be patient*. Buying resale is a rather long process, but the wait is well worth the reward. Trust me when I say that there will be days when you can't stand the wait, especially when you are waiting to see if you passed ROFR. Everyone is different—some may find it easy to wait, most will find it difficult. I consider myself a patient person, but even I grew impatient during this process. Don't be afraid to contact your sales agent if you have questions or concerns—that is what they are there for. Don't let things linger, either; if the seller is slow to sign papers, bug your agent to bug the seller. Most of the time the seller is pretty motivated because at the end of the day they just want their money, but sometimes they can be slow to sign papers.

- If there are points on the contract that are about to expire or are close to the 8-month banking deadline, try to have the seller bank them as a requirement of the sales contract. If the banking deadline passes by the time you own the contract, all is not lost. Call DVC member services and explain the situation; usually, they will make a one-time exception.

Booking

- Always try to book your home resort eleven months prior to your trip, even if you are really targeting another Walt Disney World resort. That way, if the resort you want to stay at does not have any availability at the seven-month reservations window, you have a backup plan. If you wait until the seven-month mark and don't get the resort you want, your home resort may be gone at that point, too, especially if you own at one of the smaller DVC resorts like Grand Floridian, Wilderness Lodge, or Beach Club.

- Some resorts can be hard to get into based on the time of year. Other factors such as size and location of the resort will also affect how easy it is to get a reservation. For example, the Boardwalk and Beach Club villas are very difficult to get into during Epcot's Food & Wine Festival because these resorts are within walking distance of World Showcase. The Wilderness Lodge villas and Grand Floridian villas are difficult to get into because the DVC section is quite small and in high demand year-round. Saratoga Springs, Old Key West, and Animal Kingdom Lodge are usually the easiest to reserve due to their size. There are certain room types that will be easier to get than others. For example, deluxe studios typically get reserved the quickest because they cost the least in terms of points. In general, one-bedroom villas tend to be the easiest room type to come across. Some resorts have view options on the rooms, such as standard view or lake view. Standard view rooms will go quicker that other rooms because they cost fewer points.

- If you are booking a stay that is longer than seven days, an effective strategy for making sure you get the resort is to book a seven-day trip once you enter the booking window, then each subsequent day call DVC member services and ask to add another day to your trip until you have the desired number of days. This is commonly referred to as "walking" a reservation.

- Waitlisting is a great strategy if your desired resort is not open for the dates you want. However, waitlisting multiple days is not the best idea, since all of those days would have to open up at the same time for your waitlist to be fulfilled. Instead, book the days that are available, then waitlist the additional days you need one day at a time. You can have two waitlists at once; if you need more than two days, start a new waitlist each time one comes through. It is important to waitlist weekend days first as those are usually most popular. If all of your waitlists come through, you will end up with several reservations—you can then call DVC member services and have them combine all of them into one reservation. With this strategy, you must make sure all of your waitlists and reservations match in terms of room type and view. For example, if you have a reservation at Animal Kingdom Lodge for a one-bedroom savannah view, and a second reservation at Animal Kingdom Lodge for a one-bedroom standard view, those reservations cannot be combined because they are different view types.

- Another tip to be aware of for waitlists is how they are processed. After you complete a waitlist request, it will show up in two places on your online DVC account—on your dashboard, which is the page you see after logging in, and when you click "Waitlist" under the My DVC Account dropdown. You won't be able to see where you are on the priority list; however, when someone cancels a reservation and you are next on the list, Disney's computer system will automatically put the reservation into holding so that nobody else can book it, then a DVC Cast Member periodically checks these holds and completes the reservations. This manual process can take a couple of days. When the DVC computers place the reservation in a holding status, you will notice that your waitlist will disappear from your Dashboard. If you click on "Waitlist" under the My DVC

Account dropdown, the waitlist will still show up there. This is an indication that your waitlist has come through and is in holding until a DVC reservation specialist can process it. When you see this, call member services and ask them to process the reservation. If you need to combine it with an existing reservation, you can ask them to do that while you're on the phone with them.

- Thirty days prior to your check-in date, you can complete the online check-in process and you will be able to choose up to two room requests. Room request options vary by resort, but typically they include things like upper floor, lower floor, near transportation, near elevator, and so forth. You can go one step beyond this with room requests by searching on sites like TouringPlans.com to find desirable room numbers and faxing them directly to the resort where you are staying, ideally about four days prior to your check-in date. A great place to find fax numbers for each resort is AllEars.net. While Disney doesn't guarantee that you will get what you ask for, I've found that they do try to accommodate you. I recommend you list three room numbers that you would like, in order of preference. On a recent trip I found a two-bedroom villa at Animal Kingdom Kidani Village that was technically a standard view, but had a partial view of the savannah. I faxed the request to Disney and they gave me that exact room, so I was able to save on points by getting a standard view room that still had a good view of the savannah!

- My final booking tip is to use your DVC membership to try new resorts. Each DVC resort is unique. A goal of mine is to eventually stay at each and every DVC resort, both at Walt Disney World as well as the other locations (Disneyland, Aulani, Vero Beach, and Hilton Head Island). You may just find an unexpected resort turns out to be your favorite. There are many resorts at Walt Disney World that my family would never have been able to stay at if it weren't for DVC. While we always stayed at value and moderate prior to joining DVC, we can now try those deluxe resorts that we always dreamed of visiting, but never had the financial means to do so.

During Your Trip

- First, remember that as a DVC member staying at a DVC resort, you are now "home". Cast members will go out of their way to welcome you home if they know you're a DVC member. It may seem a bit corny, but when you hear cast members welcome you home it is a great feeling.

- Take advantage of as many DVC discounts as you can. Chapter 6 details current DVC discounts, but they are constantly changing. Whenever you pay for merchandise, food, or services at Walt Disney World, don't be afraid to ask if there is a DVC discount. There have been many times when I've been surprised that there was a discount on something that I didn't even know about. On the flip side, if you ask for a DVC discount on something that you know should be discounted and the cast member says there is not a discount, don't be afraid to ask for a manager. Sometimes cast members are new or just not aware of all the discount programs.

- Take advantage of the kitchen that you have in your villa. One thing we love to do on vacation to save money is prepare breakfast in our room; then we only have to buy two meals each day (or less, depending on the size of the meal). If we're driving to Disney World, which we often do, we stop at a grocery store just outside of Disney World and pick up essentials like eggs and milk. If we're flying in, we pre-order groceries from Disney or Garden Grocer. It's a terrific way to save some money (and time). I will caution you on pre-ordering the groceries from Disney—it seems like a great idea to have them deliver the food to your room, but I've discovered that all they do is get the food from the resort store and then charge you an extra fee for delivery. You could just as easily go down to the store and get the items yourself. The prices from Garden Grocer are better, but be aware that you have to be in your room at the time of delivery—if you like to relax in your room the first day you get to Disney this is not a big deal, but if you like to head to the pool or to the parks, it may put a cramp in your style.

- Attend the free DVC member mixers. These are weekly events at the Atlantic Dance Hall at Disney's Boardwalk Inn. These mixers allow you to meet other DVC members, talk to DVC associates who can answer questions or address concerns, and enjoy free refreshments and free DVC giveaways. It's a nice way to feel more connected to the DVC community.

- If you're looking for a great place to view the Magic Kingdom fireworks, visit the Top of the World Lounge at Bay Lake Tower. This lounge is available to DVC members who are staying at any DVC resort using points. A misconception is that the lounge is only open to DVC guests at Bay Lake Tower, but this is not the case.

- When you book your DVC trip at Walt Disney World, you will get DVC member sliders to put on your MagicBands. Be sure to wear these as it identifies you to cast members who will go the extra mile to welcome you home, and it is a great way to identify to cast members that you may be eligible for a discount (don't rely on this, however; you should always ask if a discount is available to you as a DVC member). I've heard that these sliders may be going away, so if you do receive them hang onto them for future trips. While I'm not one that likes to decorate my Magic Band, I do love to wear both my DVC slider and annual passholder slider. It's a conversation piece, too. I've had many people ask me about the Disney Vacation Club during Disney bus rides because they notice the slider on my Magic Band.

- If you visit Walt Disney World once or more per year, and hate having to lug all of your stuff down every time you visit, consider getting something called an Owners Locker (OwnersLocker. com). This is a storage service that keeps your stuff in a cli-mate-controlled warehouse until you need it for your trip. When you're ready to go on your Disney trip, notify Owners Locker of your dates. and when you arrive at your hotel room the storage tote will be waiting in your room much like your luggage is wait-ing for you when you use Disney's Magical Express! Be aware that there is a one-time setup fee of $75, and then an annual membership fee of $99. The annual fee includes one storage tote (13"x20"x22") and one visit (additional visits are $25 each). You can also opt for the premium annual plan membership that includes unlimited visits for $179 per year. If you need more than one tote, there is an add-on membership of $65 per tote, per year (one visit included, additional visits are $12.50, and premium annual membership for an add-on is $139). If you are a golfer, Owner's Locker will also store you clubs for an additional fee. This is a great option if you make annual trips to Walt Disney World and want to travel a bit lighter.

- Use your DVC membership to try out new things. The discount you receive through DVC is a great reason to try a backstage tour such as Keys to the Kingdom at the Magic Kingdom or Behind the Seeds at Epcot. These tours are becoming more and more popular, and Disney continues to add new tours all the time. I had never tried a backstage tour until I was a DVC member, and now I'm hooked on them! I try to do a new tour for each trip. Do keep in mind that some backstage tours do not allow children, as Disney doesn't want to spoil the magic for the little ones. Most of the tours are walking tours, so if you have mobility issues you may want to call up Disney and ask for more details. And don't worry, they do take plenty of bathroom breaks during the tours.

EIGHT

DVC Resorts

While most people associate Walt Disney World and Disneyland with the theme parks, Disney has some of the most well-themed and beautiful resorts in the world. As a DVC member, you will be able to experience many of the best resorts that Disney has to offer. Whether the rustic and beautiful Wilderness Lodge, the Victorian elegance of the Grand Floridian, or the relaxed atmosphere of resorts like the Beach Club or Old Key West, there is a DVC resort for every taste.

One of the best parts of staying at a DVC resort is that you will truly feel at home. Disney cast members do everything possible to make you feel that way. From welcoming you home every time you walk into the resort lobby, to being available for any questions or needs you may have, the cast members at Walt Disney World really make your stay memorable.

Most of the fourteen DVC resorts are located at Walt Disney World. A few of the resorts are dedicated DVC resorts, such as Old Key West and Saratoga Springs, but most are additions to existing Disney deluxe resorts. In recent years, Disney has made it a priority to add a DVC presence at the monorail resorts near the Magic Kingdom.

In this chapter I'll give you a thorough introduction to each DVC resort, discuss each room type available, and talk about dining options. Don't be afraid to try new resorts—use your DVC membership to enjoy new experiences; I promise that you won't be disappointed!

Let's look at the Walt Disney World DVC resorts first, in the order that they opened to the public:

Disney's Old Key West Resort

Opening in 1991, Old Key West was the first Disney Vacation Club resort. It was originally known as Disney's Vacation Club Resort until

1996, when its name was changed. Old Key West is located in the Disney Springs resort area and is connected to Disney Springs via waterway, giving you the option of taking a relaxing water taxi to visit Disney's dining and shopping district. Old Key West is a dedicated DVC resort, meaning it was specifically built for DVC.

Themed after turn-of-the-century Key West, this resort is unique in that the rooms are laid out more like a condo and are some of the largest rooms available on Disney property. There are four different room types available at Old Key West, the smallest and cheapest in terms of points is the deluxe studio. The deluxe studio at Old Key West, at 390 square feet, is one of the largest DVC studios. The room has two queen beds, which is unique to Old Key West as most DVC deluxe studios have one queen bed and a double sofa sleeper. The deluxe studio room at Old Key West accommodates four guests. These rooms have one bathroom, a private porch or balcony, and a kitchenette area with a refrigerator, sink, and microwave. Deluxe studios at all DVC resorts are stocked with items like paper plates, paper bowls, paper towels, and utensils.

The next room size up is the one-bedroom villa, which is 1,005 square feet and accommodates five guests. One-bedroom villas have a king bed in the bedroom as well as a queen sofa sleeper and twin sleeper chair in the living area. Many DVC members in recent years have requested rooms that can accommodate five guests, and Disney has answered that request by adding a sleeper chair to increase guest capacity. The chair folds out similar to a sofa sleeper and is actually quite comfortable. One-bedroom villas also have one bathroom with a whirlpool tub, a separate shower, and two sinks. The room includes a washer and dryer, making extended stays more convenient, as well as a full kitchen with a refrigerator, microwave, stove, dishwasher, and dining area. The living area is generously sized. The room also includes a private porch or balcony depending on what level your room is on. Kitchens in all DVC resorts are equipped with pots and pans, cooking and eating utensils, plates, mugs, and drinking glasses. Disney provides regular and decaf coffee filter pouches for the coffee maker, as well as sugar and creamer. If there is a certain brand of coffee that you like, you may want to bring it with or purchase it after you arrive. Laundry detergent is provided, but again, if you have a specific detergent that you like to use, I recommend bringing a small amount along or buying it once you get here.

A great option if you are traveling with extended family is the next room size up—the two-bedroom villa. This room is 1,410 square feet and sleeps 9 guests. Some people are confused that many DVC resorts offer two different types of two-bedroom villas: lockoff and dedicated. The lockoff villa is essentially a one-bedroom villa and a deluxe studio with a connecting door. It has one king bed in the main bedroom (this is the "one bedroom villa" half of the room), two queen beds in the second bedroom (this is the "deluxe studio" half of the room), one queen sleeper sofa, and one twin sleeper chair. The dedicated villa has one king bed, two queen beds, one queen sleeper sofa, and one twin sleeper chair. Both types of rooms have two bathrooms, a washer and dryer, full kitchen, and a private porch or balcony.

Finally, the last and largest room type available at Old Key West is the three-bedroom grand villa. At 2,375 square feet, these rooms are huge and sleep up to 12 guests. Grand villas have one king bed, two queen beds, two full beds, and a queen sleeper sofa. The grand villa is two stories and will really make you feel like you are at a vacation home. It also features three bathrooms, a washer and dryer, full kitchen, two dining areas, and a large private porch.

One thing I love about Disney resorts is that they all have their own unique dining options. Old Key West is no different, with four dining options to choose from. Olivia's Café is a table-service restaurant that offers breakfast, lunch, and dinner. Good's Food to Go is a counter-service restaurant near the feature pool and is open for breakfast lunch and dinner. The Gurgling Suitcase is a bar that offers drinks and simple snacks. The Turtle Shack is another counter-service location that is near the village pool; it is open seasonally and has a smaller selection than Good's Food to Go.

If you are looking for a relaxing atmosphere and room to spread out, then Old Key West is the place for you. Being the first DVC resort, Disney tried to make Old Key West much more of a condo-type resort. Another unique aspect of Old Key West is that only three of its 49 three-story buildings have elevators (buildings 62, 63, and 64). If you have mobility issues, or just don't like stairs, request a ground floor room or make sure you get one of the three buildings with elevators.

Old Key West is large and spread-out, so if you're using Disney's bus transportation, you'll want to allow extra time as there are several bus stops throughout this sprawling resort. If you have a car, you may be better off driving—especially if you have to get somewhere for a dinner reservation. As we mentioned earlier, there is also boat transportation to Disney Springs.

One of the most unique aspects of Old Key West is that it really has a community feel to it. As the oldest DVC resort, many DVC members who call this their home resort have been members for over 20 years and tend to come to this resort over and over, often for long periods of time, so over the years many of them have gotten to know each other. So there are a lot of friends that vacation here at the same time, and many of them know the Old Key West cast members very well.

The best phrase I can use to sum up Disney's Old Key West resort is "laid back". The points required to stay here are toward the lower end of the spectrum, so it can be a great value, especially when you consider the larger-than-average room sizes. If you have kids, you may want to think about staying at one of the other DVC resorts. Old Key West is a great resort, but does seem to be geared a bit more toward adults. As with all Disney resorts, it all depends on your taste—Old Key West has plenty of positives, but I wouldn't recommend staying here for your first DVC trip. Check it out first and then decide then if you want to try it out on a future trip.

Disney's Boardwalk Villas

Located on Crescent Lake near World Showcase in Epcot, the Boardwalk Villas opened with the rest of the Boardwalk resort in 1996. The Boardwalk is styled after Atlantic Coast resorts of the 1930s, and it's extremely popular during Epcot's Food & Wine festival due to its close proximity to Epcot's International Gateway Entrance, which is located in between France and the UK in World Showcase. While its proximity to Epcot is great, it is also very close to Hollywood Studios. There is a walking trail leading from the Epcot resort area to Hollywood Studios. If walking is not your thing, there's also a boat connecting the Boardwalk resort to Hollywood Studios.

When Disney built the Boardwalk, they started to design DVC rooms more like large hotel rooms rather than the condo-style rooms at Old Key West. There are four different room types available at the Boardwalk Villas. The entry-level room is the deluxe studio, which is 359 square feet and sleeps four guests. The room has one queen bed, one full sleeper sofa, one bathroom, a kitchenette, and a private porch or balcony. Three different views are available: standard, garden, or BoardWalk. The standard view requires the fewest number of points and tends to book up the fastest, while the other views will cost more, but may have better availability. Disney is refurbishing this resort in 2015, and will be adding a pull-down bunk bed to the rooms so that they can accommodate five guests—great news for families with three kids!

The one-bedroom villa at Boardwalk is 712 square feet and sleeps four guests. The room has one king bed and one queen sleeper sofa. Disney does allow one extra guest in this room type, but you will only have linens for four guests, and they do not provide cots or roll-aways, so you will need to plan accordingly by bringing an air mattress or sleeping bag if you do have five guests. One-bedroom villas have one bathroom with a whirlpool tub, a separate shower, and two sinks. The room includes a washer and dryer, full kitchen, dining area, living area, and two balconies

The two-bedroom villa at the Boardwalk is 1072 square feet, accommodates eight guests, and is only available in a lockoff configuration. The room features one king bed, one queen bed, one queen sleeper sofa, one full sleeper sofa, two bathrooms, a washer and dryer, full kitchen, and living area. There are also three private balconies to enjoy, one off the main bedroom, one off the living area, and one of the second bedroom. The two-bedroom villas are available as a standard, garden, or BoardWalk view.

The three-bedroom grand villa, at 2142 square feet, is the largest room type available at the Boardwalk. This room can accommodate up to twelve guests and features one king bed, four queen beds, one queen sleeper sofa, three bathrooms, washer and dryer, full kitchen, huge dining and living area, and a gigantic balcony that spans the entire width of the villa with doors off of each bedroom as well as the living and dining areas. The grand villa is available as a standard, garden, or BoardWalk view.

The Boardwalk is arguably one of the best DVC resorts for recreation and dining. It has three pools—the Luna Park feature pool and two quiet pools. The Luna Park pool is themed after an early 1900s carnival and includes a 200-foot water slide known as the Keister Coaster. I must warn you that if you are not a fan of clowns, you may want to stay away from the Luna Park Pool as the theming does involve clowns. There are also quiet pools located both on the inn side of the resort as well as the DVC villas side of the resort. Also located near the feature pool is the Luna Park Crazy House, a play area for children. If you're looking for great nightlife, then the Boardwalk is definitely for you. The Atlantic Dance Hall is located on the far end of the villas and is a classic dance hall open to guests 21 and over. Jellyrolls is another great adult venue, featuring a dueling piano bar. Like the Atlantic Dance Hall, you must be 21 or over to visit Jellyrolls. A good recreation option at the Boardwalk is renting surrey bikes (four-wheeled peddle cars) or standard bicycles and navigating around the sprawling BoardWalk area (which also includes Disney's Yacht & Beach Club resorts).

You have several dining options available to you at the Boardwalk resort. Big River Grille & Brewing Works is on the villas side of the resort and offers classic American dishes for lunch and dinner. The Flying Fish Café is located on the inn side of the resort and is one of the best locations at Walt Disney World for seafood. Trattorio al Forno is a fairly new, upscale restaurant that features great Italian cuisine. The ESPN Club offers classic American lunch and dinner items in a sports bar-type setting. There are several kiosks and food carts along the BoardWalk itself offering favorites like pizza, churros, popcorn, and both alcoholic and non-alcoholic drinks. Since the BoardWalk is located on Crescent Lake, there are several other resorts and dining locations that are just a short walk or boat ride away at the Yacht and Beach Club resorts, Swan & Dolphin Resorts, and Epcot's World Showcase.

The Boardwalk is the only Disney resort to have its own entertainment district, sitting along a quarter-mile long, authentic boardwalk similar to Coney Island in New York. Guests can enjoy plenty of recreation as well as classic street performers and midway games. There's plenty of shopping to enjoy at the Boardwalk resort as well. Located inside the resort, Dundry's Sundries sells resort merchandise as well as basic sundries. Screen Door General Store, Disney's Character Carnival, and Thimbles and Threads are all located in a large store to the left of the BoardWalk promenade. These stores offer a wide variety of food, merchandise, postcards, and collector pins. You'll also find clothes and novelty items. If sports are more your thing, the ESPN Club store is located on the inn side of the Boardwalk resort, offering your favorite team merchandise. The ESPN Club store also shares space with a video arcade that kids and young-at-heart adults will love.

The Boardwalk is a beautiful and amazingly-themed resort. It is located in a prime area—close to both Epcot and Hollywood Studios—and it is a great value in terms of DVC points. This is a resort that is appealing to adults and children alike. If you've never tried the Boardwalk resort before, becoming a DVC member is a great way to start.

The Villas at Disney's Wilderness Lodge

The Wilderness Lodge opened in 1994 and the DVC villas were built as a separate add-on building to the resort six years later in 2000. Wilderness Lodge Villas, in terms of number of rooms, is the second smallest of Walt Disney World's DVC properties. While the main Wilderness Lodge building is themed after national park lodges of the Pacific Northwest, the villas building is themed after lodgings built by those working on the transcontinental railroad. Walt Disney was a train enthusiast, so it only made sense to have a resort themed after railroading.

There are only three different room types available at the Wilderness Lodge Villas. The deluxe studio is 356 square feet and, after a recent renovation, accommodates up to five guests. It has one queen bed, one full sleeper sofa, one twin pull-down bunk, one bathroom, a kitchenette, and a private porch or balcony. The recent renovation of the Wilderness Lodge Villas increased guest capacity in the studio to five guests with the addition of a pull-down twin bunk. It is one of only a handful of DVC resorts that offers five-guest capacity in a deluxe studio, a trend that will no doubt continue as more DVC resorts are built, and as existing DVC resorts are refurbished.

The one-bedroom villa is 727 square feet and accommodates up to four guests. This room has one king bed and one queen sleeper sofa. Similar to the Boardwalk, Disney allows one extra guest in this room type, but you will only have linens for four guests. One-bedroom villas have one bathroom with a whirlpool tub, a separate shower, and two sinks. The room includes a washer and dryer, full kitchen, dining area, living area, and one balcony or porch off of the living room.

The two-bedroom villa is 1080 square feet and sleeps 8 guests. This room is available in both lockoff and dedicated configurations. The lockoff room has one king bed, one queen bed, one queen sleeper sofa, and one full sleeper sofa. The dedicated villa has one king bed, two queen beds, and one queen sleeper sofa. Both types of rooms feature two bathrooms, washer and dryer, full kitchen, dining area, and living area. Two-bedroom villas have two separate balconies, one off of the second bedroom and one off of the living room.

Disney's Wilderness Lodge Resort is viewed by many to be Disney's most majestic resort. With its awe-inspiring lobby and its wonderfully themed feature pool area, Wilderness Lodge will truly immerse you in its theme—you will no longer feel like you are in central Florida but rather in the Pacific Northwest. The villas building is much more intimate and quiet, and holds a special place in the heart of many Walt Disney fans because it is home to the Carolwood Pacific Room, a mini-museum featuring Walt Disney's love of trains. The room features photographs, replicas, and actual artifacts from Walt Disney's backyard railroad, which he named the Carolwood Pacific.

A quiet pool is situated next to the villas building, but there are no dining options in that building; all dining is located in the main lodge. Roaring Forks offers a limited counter-service fare. The Territory Lounge is one of the best lounges in all of Walt Disney World. It offers both alcoholic and non-alcoholic beverages as well as several unique and delicious appetizers and snacks. The Territory Lounge is a great option if you don't have an ADR (advanced dining reservation) or want a more laid-back, relaxed atmosphere. You can actually make a meal out of eating at the lounge by ordering a sampling of appetizers for your table—it's a great way to save a little money at Walt Disney World.

In terms of table service dining, there are two options at Wilderness Lodge. The Whispering Canyon Café is a family-style table service restaurant. Despite its name, it is a very loud and interactive dining experience—the wait staff will ensure that you have a rip-roaring great time here! If you want something a little bit quieter and upscale, the feature restaurant at Wilderness Lodge is Artist Point. This is a great place to celebrate a special occasion; it's a breathtaking restaurant that serves food typically found in America's Northwest, including specialties like cedar plank salmon and grilled buffalo.

Wilderness Lodge is one of the most beautiful and visually stunning resorts on Walt Disney World property. As with all of the Magic Kingdom area resorts, it is meant to parallel a land at the Magic Kingdom—in this case, Frontierland. Wilderness Lodge holds a special place in my heart for a couple of different reasons. First, my parents took us during our spring breaks camping at Fort Wilderness, which is right next door and themed similarly to Wilderness Lodge. There is a beautiful walking trail that connects the two resorts. I can remember taking boat rides on Bay Lake and watching cranes lift huge logs into place as they were building this beautiful resort. The other reason it holds a special place in my heart is because it's where my wife and I spent part of our honeymoon.

As many times as I have visited Wilderness Lodge, every time I enter that lobby it takes my breath away—I could sit there for hours. There are so many hidden treasures there. When I was a teenager, I was exploring this resort and found a great fireplace area on the second floor with a small seating area in front of it. Nobody was there, and it was so relaxing to sit by that fire. Who would think that sitting by a fireplace at a resort in Florida would be so appealing, even if it might be 100 degrees outside with 100% humidity! But that's the essence of Wilderness Lodge. I don't know if there is another Disney resort that so immerses you in its atmosphere. It is certainly worth a visit during your Disney World trip. Spend an afternoon or evening, make a reservation at Artist Point or Whispering Canyon—you won't be sorry.

As far as DVC points requirements for staying here, Wilderness Lodge is in the middle of the pack—you will need about the same number of points to stay here as the Beach Club, but fewer than at the other Magic Kingdom DVC resorts, which makes it a great deal if you want to be near the Magic Kingdom. Snagging a reservation can be difficult, as it is one of the smaller DVC resorts, but never fear, Disney has recently announced plans to increase the number of rooms very soon, as well as plans to build waterfront cabins along the Bay Lake shoreline. This resort has always been popular among DVC owners, and I don't foresee that changing anytime soon.

Disney's Beach Club Villas

The Beach Club Villas opened in 2002 as an add-on to the popular Beach Club Resort that opened 12 years earlier in 1990. The villas are designed to reflect the whimsical architecture of oceanfront homes that were built in the early 20th century in Cape May, New Jersey. Similar to the Boardwalk Villas, the Beach Club Villas are quite popular during Epcot's Food & Wine Festival in September and October, so you may need a little bit of luck and pixie dust to get a reservation here during the fall. One of the best features of this resort is its proximity to Epcot—it is literally steps away from Epcot's International Gateway entrance.

Similar to Wilderness Lodge, there are only three types of DVC villas offered at the Beach Club. First is the deluxe studio, which is 365 square feet and accommodates up to four guests, with one queen bed and one full sleeper sofa. The room features one bathroom, a kitchenette, and a private porch or balcony. The Beach Club is going to be undergoing a refurbishment in 2016 that will increase the studio capacity to five guests with the addition of a twin pull-down bunk.

One-bedroom villas are 726 square feet and accommodate up to four guests. There is one king bed and one queen sleeper sofa, along with one bathroom, a washer and dryer, full kitchen, dining area and living area. The room also features one private porch or balcony off of the living area.

Two-bedroom villas are 1083 square feet and accommodate up to eight guests. Lockoff rooms have one king bed, one queen bed, one queen sleeper sofa, and one full sleeper sofa. Dedicated rooms have one king bed, two queen beds, and one queen sleeper sofa. Both room types have two bathrooms, a washer and dryer, full kitchen, dining area, and living area. There are two private porches or balconies, one off of the living area and one off of the second bedroom.

The Beach Club has become one of my favorite DVC resorts. I love the theming and relaxed feeling. A huge bonus of staying at the Beach Club Villas is access to Stormalong Bay, a pool area that is shared between the Beach Club and Yacht Club resorts. Stormalong Bay is really more of a small water park than a pool—it has several water slides, a huge and winding sand bottom pool, and it even has its own lazy river. The quiet pool located adjacent to the villas building is a great place to relax and unwind after a day at the parks, and it has a gigantic hot tub that is seldom crowded.

The Beach Club is a great resort for dining. Cape May Café is a table-service restaurant that offers breakfast and dinner, and has one of the best and most reasonable character breakfasts on all of Disney property. Characters featured at the Cape May Café character breakfast include Minnie, Donald, Daisy, Goofy, Pluto, and sometimes Mickey. In the evening, Cape May offers a terrific seafood buffet that includes crab legs on select nights. Another great table service location is the Beaches & Cream Soda Shop, a 50s style diner that serves American food and ice cream. One of the specialties at Beaches & Cream is the kitchen sink sundae—see if you and your table mates will be able to finish this huge ice-cream dessert! Beaches & Cream is a rather small restaurant, so it can be difficult to obtain an ADR here, and especially difficult to get walkup seating. Your best bet, if you don't have a reservation, is to order carryout. Hurricane Hanna's is a poolside counter-service restaurant offering typical American fare as well as drinks. The Beach Club Marketplace is a quick-service location with a limited menu of hot items, as well as snacks and drinks. You can go next door to the Yacht Club Resort to get one of the best steaks on Disney property at the Yachtsman Steakhouse. Or, you can take a short walk over to Epcot's World Showcase to enjoy the wide variety of foods there. Plus, the Beach Club shares the promenade not only with the Yacht Club resort, but also the Boardwalk Resort and entertainment district, so you can take advantage of all the experiences we talked about a little while ago at the Boardwalk.

There are so many reasons to love Disney's Beach Club Villas. It has quickly jumped to the top of my list and become my favorite DVC resort. You just can't beat its location, especially in the fall during Epcot's Food & Wine Festival. I find the Yacht Club resort can feel a little "stuffy", but the Beach Club Resort—and the DVC villas building in particular—has a completely different feel to it. It is so much quieter, serene, and laid back. The Beach Club resort is in the middle of the pack as far as points cost. It is roughly equivalent to Wilderness Lodge and slightly more than the Boardwalk. You simply can't go wrong staying at Disney's Beach Club Villas!

Disney's Saratoga Springs Resort & Spa

Saratoga Springs holds the distinction of being the largest Disney Vacation Club resort. It was built in four phases on the former site of the Disney Institute. The resort has an equestrian theme and is modeled after the city of Saratoga Springs, New York. This is a gigantic resort, occupying 65 acres and having 1260 rooms plus 60 treehouse villas. Phase one of Disney's Saratoga Springs Resort opened in 2004 and the final phase, the Treehouse Villas, opened in 2009.

Saratoga Springs has five different types of rooms. Deluxe studios are pretty standard and clock in at 365 square feet. The deluxe studio can accommodate up to 4 guests with one queen bed and one full sleeper sofa. The room has one bathroom, a kitchenette, and a private porch or balcony.

The next room size up from the deluxe studio is the one-bedroom villa. One bedrooms are 714 square feet and accommodate up to four guests. Disney will allow five guests in a one bedroom, but linens and bedding will only be provided for four guests. The room has a spacious bedroom with one king bed and a living area with one queen sleeper sofa, one bathroom, a washer and dryer, full kitchen, dining area, and living area. There is a large private porch or balcony located off of the living area and bedroom.

Two-bedroom villas are 1,075 square feet, can accommodate up to eight guests, and are available in two different configurations. Lockoff villas have one king bed, one queen bed, one queen sleeper sofa, and one full sleeper sofa. Dedicated villas have one king bed, two queen beds, and one queen sleeper sofa. Both types of rooms have two bathrooms, a washer and dryer, full kitchen, dining area, and living area. Dedicated villas have one porch or balcony located off of the living area, while lockoff villas will have one large porch or balcony spanning the living area and main bedroom.

Unique to Saratoga Springs are the Treehouse Villas. These villas are secluded in the forest along the Sassagoula River next to the main resort and sit ten feet off the ground. These rustic cabins are 1074 square feet and sleep nine guests. While the treehouses may look rustic from the outside, they are quite nice on the inside, with upscale features like cathedral ceilings and granite countertops. There are two queen beds, one twin bunk bed, one queen sleeper sofa, and one twin sleeper chair. The treehouses have two bathrooms, a washer and dryer, full kitchen, dining area, large living area, and private deck.

The three-bedroom grand villa is the largest room type available. It is 2113 square feet, occupies two levels, and can accommodate up to twelve guests. The room features one king bed, four queen beds, one queen sleeper sofa, four bathrooms, a washer and dryer, full kitchen, huge dining and living area, and a porch off of the dining area.

The sheer size of Saratoga Springs can be overwhelming, but it is a beautiful resort and is especially great for golfers since it sits adjacent to the Lake Buena Vista golf course. Its proximity to Disney

Springs is also a great feature—Disney recently opened a pedestrian bridge that makes it an easy walk from the Congress Park area of Saratoga Springs. There are six unique sections within the resort, each with its own unique feel.

The Springs is closest to the lobby, main restaurants, and feature pool. Being the closest to the main hub of the resort, it's best for families with kids or those with mobility issues. Another great section for families is the Paddock, which is home to Saratoga Springs' second feature pool as well as additional counter-service dining. The Paddock is somewhat spread out, so this may not be the best area if you have mobility issues. Adjacent to the Paddock, the Carousel is the smallest section and does not have its own pool like the other sections do. The fourth section, Congress Park, is closest to Disney Springs and has its own quiet pool. Congress Park is a great section to stay at if you are vacationing with adults only. Finally, the Grandstand includes regular villa rooms and has its own quiet pool.

The most recently completed section of Saratoga Springs, and the area that really almost feels like a separate resort unto itself, is the Treehouse Villas. You can walk from them to the main resort, but it is a fairly long walk, so it may be better to take transportation or even use your car if you have one. The Treehouse Villas do feature their own quiet pool, but there are no dining options.

Dining options are limited at Saratoga Springs. The Artist's Palette is a market-style counter-service restaurant that offers sandwiches, grab-and-go items, and daily dinner features. While it is a small counter service location, they offer some great items like flatbread sandwiches as well as a feature of the day. The Turf Club Bar & Grill is a full-service restaurant and lounge area; however, only dinner is served. The Turf Club also has a great lounge where you can enjoy both alcoholic and non-alcoholic beverages, as well as a limited appetizer and snack menu. The Paddock Grill is a poolside bar at the Paddock Pool with a fairly lengthy counter-service menu. On the Rocks is a poolside bar by the High Rock Springs feature pool. The Backstretch Pool Bar at the Grandstand Pool has drinks and light meals/snacks.

While dining options at Saratoga Springs are somewhat limited, it is important to remember that the resort is right next to Disney Springs, which has many places to eat. Disney Springs will continue to get more dining locations as Disney transforms it from what used to be Downtown Disney.

Similar to Old Key West, Saratoga Springs doesn't have the immersive theming of a typical Walt Disney World Resort, but some may find it appealing—especially adults. I do feel, however, that this is a great location for both adults and kids. My children loved the main pool area here; it was tough to get them out of the water!

Saratoga Springs is also home to the Disney Vacation Club information center, the official sales hub of DVC. Here you will find a preview lobby as well as several full-scale models of DVC rooms, including rooms from the latest DVC resort(s) that Disney has for sale, not just Saratoga Springs rooms. You can meet with a DVC sales associate who can answer any of your questions. They also have transportation available so the sales associate can take you to visit a DVC property. If you are on the fence about DVC, or even if you plan to buy resale, the DVC information center may merit a visit.

One somewhat unique feature that Saratoga Spring can boast is that it's one of only two Disney resorts at Walt Disney World that has a full-service spa (the other is Disney's Grand Floridian Resort & Spa). (There is actually another spa located at the Swan and Dolphin resorts, but they are not Disney owned.) Keep in mind that if you don't stay at Saratoga Springs, you can still use the spa. Spa treatments can be a great way to make your trip extra special. Couples spa treatments are available, or if your spouse enjoys spa treatments and you enjoy golf, Saratoga Springs offers you the best of both worlds, And don't forget to get your DVC discount. There are also tons of trails around the resort, if you like to walk, jog, or run, and you can rent bikes here to navigate the many trails.

Saratoga Springs is a beautiful resort and one that I think is overlooked and underrated. Some may say it is a little light on theming compared to the other Disney World resorts, but I think Saratoga Springs has a lot of character. Maybe I'm being prejudiced because this is a home resort for me, but I do like it. Speaking of home resorts, if you are looking for a resale contract I think a contract at Saratoga Springs offers the best value—that's exactly why I bought into this resort after finishing all of my DVC research. What makes it such a great candidate? Several reasons. First, the price-per-point is pretty low compared to other home resorts, even the ones that have expiration dates in 2042 (the expiration date at Saratoga Springs is 2054). The yearly maintenance fees are also very low, in fact; they are the second lowest of all Disney World DVC resorts (the only one that's cheaper is Bay Lake Tower, but your price-per-point cost will be much more there). Being that this is our home resort, it was also the resort we chose for our first DVC resort stay, and my entire family loved it.

In terms of points required to stay here, Saratoga Springs is in the middle of the pack compared to other Disney World DVC resorts. It's on par with DVC resorts like Wilderness Lodge and Beach Club. I believe Saratoga Springs is going to grow much more popular in the coming years as Disney completes the re-imagining of Downtown Disney into Disney Springs. While this will add more shopping and dining to the area, the new Disney Springs area fits in very well with Saratoga Springs in terms of theming. Although many complain of the lack of theming, I think Disney had its eye on the future with Saratoga Springs.

Disney's Animal Kingdom Villas—Jambo House

The Animal Kingdom Lodge was opened in 2001 and expanded in 2008 to include 109 DDVC Villas on the upper floors of the original lodge building, now known as Jambo House. This resort is six stories tall and has a majestic open lobby that is somewhat akin to Wilderness Lodge. Jambo House has an African theme and sits adjacent to savannahs with grazing wildlife, allowing guests to view animals from their balconies (if they have a savannah-view room). While the resort sits next to the Animal Kingdom theme park, the savannahs at the lodge are separate from the park. Most room types are available as either a standard view or savannah view, with savannah view rooms costing more in terms of points.

Studios at Jambo House are unique in that they actually fall into two different categories: value and deluxe. Value studios are 316 square feet; deluxe studios are 356 square feet. Both rooms accommodate up to four guests with one queen bed and one full sleeper sofa. Both rooms also have one bathroom, a kitchenette, and a private balcony.

One-bedroom villas are also available as either value or standard. Value rooms are 629 square feet and accommodate up to four guests with one king bed and one queen sleeper sofa. Standard rooms are 802 square feet and accommodate up to five guests (with the addition of a twin sleeper chair in the living area). Both types of rooms have one bedroom, a washer and dryer, full kitchen, dining area, and living area. A private porch spans both the living area and main bedroom.

Two-bedroom villas are also available as both value and standard. Value rooms have 945 square feet and accommodate up to eight guests with one king bed, one queen bed, one queen sleeper sofa, and one full sleeper sofa. Standard rooms are 1173 square feet and accommodate up to nine guests with the addition of a twin sleeper chair in the living area. Both rooms have two bathrooms, a washer and dryer, full kitchen, dining area, living area, and a private balcony spanning the entire width of the villa—main bedroom, living area, and second bedroom.

Three-bedroom grand villas are 2201 square feet and accommodate up to twelve guests with one king bed, four queen beds, and one queen sofa sleeper. The room features three-and-a-half bathrooms, a washer and dryer, full kitchen, and huge living and dining area. Private balconies are located off of each bedroom and the living area.

Jambo House at the Animal Kingdom Lodge has many dining options. The Mara is a food court with a wide variety of foods to satisfy anyone's palette, whether you are adventurous or not so adventurous. Jiko—The Cooking Place is a unique table-service restaurant featuring African style cooking. The tables in the dining room surround an open kitchen. Boma—Flavors of Africa is a buffet-style restaurant featuring many unique and delicious dishes. Many consider Boma to be one of the best all-you-can-eat dining experiences at Walt Disney World, mainly due to its unique foods and variety. Boma is great, but it can also be extremely crowded, making getting your food a chore in itself. If you plan to dine at Boma, budget plenty of time. There is also a bar located near the Uzima Springs Pool.

Animal Kingdom Lodge features the largest pool on Disney property—the Uzima Springs Pool, at 11,000 square feet, with zero-depth entry, a 67-foot long slide, kids wading pool, and kids play area. The pool is open 24 hours, but lifeguards go off-duty at 10pm. While there is no quiet pool at Animal Kingdom Lodge, there are two hot tubs near the Uzima Springs Pool. A unique recreational activity offered at the lodge is nightly African storytelling near Ogun's Firepit. The storytelling is held every night regardless of weather; in case of inclement weather, the storytelling will be moved inside the resort.

While Animal Kingdom Lodge is farther away from the rest of Walt Disney World—particularly the Magic Kingdom, Epcot, and Hollywood Studios—some may view this as an advantage, for the resort as it feels a little bit more secluded than most other resorts on Disney property. Animal Kingdom Lodge is one of the best points values among DVC resorts. Jambo House is the only DVC resort to offer a "value studio", but these can be awfully hard to get, especially if it is not your home resorts, because there are a limited number of them available.

If you love animals, or plan to spend a good deal of time at the Animal Kingdom theme park during your stay, then Animal Kingdom Lodge is a great place for youy. The rooms are very nice and well-appointed. Some folks are a little frightened by eating here, thinking all they have is strange foods, but there is something for everyone. I was pleasantly surprised on my first visit.

Disney's Animal Kingdom Villas—Kidani Village

An additional DVC-only section of the Animal Kingdom Lodge, named Kidani Village, opened in 2009 with more than 300 villas. Once Kidani Village opened, the main lodge was renamed Jambo House to distinguish between the two areas. The savannahs from the main lodge were extended to Kidani Village, and one additional savannah was added. Kidani Village shares theming with Jambo House, but it really does feel like its own resort, which is why I decided to devote a separate section to it.

Kidani Village has four different types of rooms, starting with the deluxe studio which, at 366 square feet, can accommodate four guests with one queen bed and one full sleeper sofa. The room also includes one bathroom and a kitchenette. The rooms have a private balcony and are available as either standard or savannah view. Value studios are not offered at Kidani Village; they are only offered at Jambo House. In general, for all room types, standard-view rooms will book up quicker than savannah-view rooms due to the points cost.

One-bedroom villas are 807 square feet and accommodate up to five guests with one king bed, one queen sleeper sofa, and one twin sleeper chair. One of the great features about staying in a one-bedroom villa at Kidani Village is that it has two bathrooms, which can be a benefit when trying to get out the door early to make rope drop at the parks. The room also includes a full kitchen, washer and dryer, dining area, and living area. The private balcony spans the entire width of the room and has entrances from both the bedroom and living area. Like the deluxe studio, this room is also available as either a standard view or savannah view.

Two-bedroom villas are 1152 square feet and can accommodate up to nine guests. They are available as either a lockoff villa, with one king bed, one queen bed, one queen sleeper sofa, one full sleeper sofa, and one twin sleeper chair; or as a dedicated room with one king bed, two queen beds, one full sleeper sofa, and one twin sleeper chair. Staying in a two-bedroom villa gives you three bathrooms, a washer and dryer, full kitchen, dining area, and living area. Private balconies in these villas are huge, spanning the entire width of the room with entrances from both bedrooms and the living area. Two bedrooms are also available as either a standard view or savannah view.

Three-bedroom grand villas are a whopping 2349 square feet and accommodate up to twelve guests, with one king bed, four queen beds, and one queen sleeper sofa. These rooms have two levels. The lower level has a master suite, two bathrooms, kitchen, dining area, and living area. The second floor has two bedrooms, each having their own private bathroom, and another living area. The grand villa also has a washer and dryer and three balconies. The lower-level balcony spans the entire width of the room with entrances from the master suite, living area, and dining area. The two second-floor balconies are located off of the two bedrooms. These rooms are also available as either a standard view or savannah view.

Kidani Village does not have as many dining options as Jambo House. Sanaa, a table-service restaurant on the lower level of Kidani Village, is the only restaurant here. Overlooking the savannah, Sanaa offers spectacular views of the animals as well as tasty food from tandoor ovens. If you're looking for something a little more laid back, Sanaa has a great lounge where you can kick back, relax, and enjoy a beverage (both alcoholic and non-alcoholic) and an appetizer or snack. Drinks and other snacks can be purchased at both the pool bar and the Kidani Village lobby. There is a shuttle that transports guests back and forth between Jambo House and Kidani Village, so you do have the option of eating at one of the Jambo House restaurants. There is also a small marketplace inside the lobby of Kidani Village where you can buy merchandise as well as a limited selection of grocery items.

Kidani Village is unique in that parking is located underneath the resort, which adds to its immersive, savannah feel as everyone's car is out of site. Even though I'm not big on animals, and Animal

Kingdom is my least favorite theme park, I really do enjoy staying at Kidani Village; it's a relaxing and serene resort. The rooms are breathtaking and there's nothing better than sitting on your balcony and looking out over the beautiful savannah, especially when the animals are grazing. I was pleasantly surprised by how much wildlife we saw. Even if you don't have a savannah-view room, there are many observation areas where you can sit and watch the wildlife, and there are always cast members around that can help you identify animals and tell you more about their homeland. Kidani Village has its own pool that features zero entry as well as a long waterslide.

Kidani Village is a great resort for both adults and kids. Much like Wilderness Lodge, Animal Kingdom Lodge has a totally immersive feel to it—you'll feel like you are no longer in central Florida. Plus, there are plenty of activities for the kids that are both fun and edu-cational. In fact, my kids had so much fun with the activities that I don't think they even realized they were actually learning some-thing. Transportation at the Animal Kingdom Lodge is limited to buses, and while the Animal Kingdom theme park is mere minutes away, the other three theme parks are a good distance off, so you're going to have to allow plenty of time in your trip plan, especially if you have a dining reservation.

Both the Jambo House and Kidani Village sections of Animal Kingdom Lodge are beautiful and wonderfully themed, though I prefer Kidani Village to Jambo House. It has a welcoming atmo-sphere that makes you feel totally at home. Rooms at the Animal Kingdom Lodge are a great value in terms of DVC points, mostly due to its remote location away from the Magic Kingdom and Epcot.

Bay Lake Tower (Disney's Contemporary Resort)

Opening in 2009, Bay Lake Tower sits next to Disney's iconic Contemporary Resort, on the land formerly occupied by the north wing of the Contemporary. Bay Lake Tower shares the Contemporary's modern theming and is connected to the Contemporary by a covered pedestrian walkway. The Contemporary was the first monorail resort to receive a DVC addition.

Bay Lake Tower offers four different types of rooms. The deluxe studio is 339 square feet and accommodates up to four guests with one queen bed and one full sleeper sofa. The room has one bathroom, a kitchenette, and a private porch or balcony. These rooms are available as a standard view, lake view, or theme park view (overlooking the Magic Kingdom). The studios at Bay Lake Tower are very small with a somewhat awkward bathroom/kitchenette layout. I recommend choosing a larger room if you want to stay at this resort.

One-bedroom villas are 803 square feet and sleep up to five guests with one king bed, one queen sleeper sofa, and one twin sleeper chair. Like the rooms at Animal Kingdom Kidani, these one-bedroom villas also have two bathrooms—a lifesaver when trying to get out of the door to make rope drop at the theme parks. These rooms also have a washer and dryer, full kitchen, dining area, and living area. A small balcony off of the bedroom is included, and the room has the same view options as the deluxe studio (standard, lake, and theme park).

Two-bedroom villas are offered in both lockoff or dedicated layouts. The rooms have 1152 square feet and sleep up to nine guests. Lockoff villas have one king bed, one queen bed, one queen sleeper sofa, one full sleeper sofa, and one twin sleeper chair. Dedicated villas have one king bed, two queen beds, one queen sleeper sofa, and one twin sleeper chair. Additional features of these rooms include three bathrooms, a washer and dryer, full kitchen, dining area, living area, and two private porches or balconies—one off of each bedroom. Again, these rooms are available as a standard, lake, or theme park view.

Three-bedroom grand villas are 2044 square feet and sleep twelve guests with one king bed, four queen beds, and one queen sleeper sofa. These rooms are laid out very similarly to Animal Kingdom Kidani's grand villas, except that there are four balconies—one off of each bedroom and one off of the first floor dining area. The room includes a washer and dryer, full kitchen, dining area, and two living areas. Grand villas are available with the same view options as the other rooms at Bay Lake Tower: standard, lake, and theme park.

Bay Lake Tower has a unique, semi-circular design, giving the rooms a unique wedge shape. The resort matches the modern theming of the Contemporary and is meant to tie into Tomorrowland—the land at the Magic Kingdom that the resort sits closest to. If you're a Magic Kingdom fan, then Bay Lake Tower may just be the resort for you due to its close proximity to the park. At the end of a long day at the Magic Kingdom, there's nothing like being able to bypass the crowded buses and just walk back to your resort. Being attached to one of the most iconic Disney resort has its benefits too.

There's plenty of recreation and dining here to enjoy. Bay Lake Tower has its own pool, water playground, pool bar, and bocce ball courts in the courtyard of the resort. Over at the Contemporary you can enjoy another pool area as well as a marina with boat rentals. Transportation options at Bay Lake Tower include monorail, bus, and boat. If you're looking for even more recreation, Fort Wilderness is a short boat ride away and offers hiking, canoeing, archery, bike rentals, and much more.

Bay Lake Tower is home to the Top of The World Lounge, which sits atop the building and features an outdoor viewing deck for the Magic Kingdom fireworks as well as an indoor seating area with a full bar and limited menu. The Top of the World Lounge features views of the Magic Kingdom as well as other surrounding resorts. All Bay Lake Tower guests can visit the lounge's viewing deck until 4pm, but from 5pm until midnight only DVC members staying on a DVC points reservation can come here. During the Magic Kingdom fireworks, the theme park soundtrack is played both in the lounge and on the outside viewing deck. If you are a DVC member, you must visit this lounge at least once.

Other dining options that are a short walk away inside the Contemporary's main building include the California Grill, Chef Mickey's, The Wave...of American Flavors, and the Contempo Cafe. While the Top of the World Lounge offers the best views of the Magic Kingdom Fireworks, California Grill is a close second. California Grill is a signature table-service restaurant featuring steaks and seafood. It's a great place to celebrate special occasions, especially if you can get one of the coveted reservations around the time of the fireworks. Even if you dine here a couple of hours before the fireworks, the wait staff will understand if you want to stretch your dinner out to catch the fireworks—just let them know and they won't rush you. The Contemporary is also home to one of the most sought-after character meals at Walt Disney World—Chef Mickey's. Getting a reservation here can sometimes be difficult, but most Disney fans will agree that it is a "must do" at least once. A restaurant that is one of my personal favorites is The Wave, located next to the check-in area at the Contemporary (this is also the former location of the Fiesta Fun Center arcade, which many of us 80s and 90s kids will remember from all of the quarters spent here). The Wave is a great place to dine that offers a lot of fresh options, most of which are sourced locally. It has great food, a casual atmosphere, and a lounge where you can relax and get a drink or appetizer. The Contempo Café is a quick-service dining location that offers snacks, drinks, and lighter fare. Finally, the Outer Rim is a great lounge located in the Contemporary's grand concourse—enjoy a drink or two and an appetizer here while the monorails whiz by above.

The amount of points required to stay at Bay Lake Tower are toward the high end of the spectrum for Walt Disney World DVC resorts, especially if you want a room with a theme park view.

The Villas at Disney's Grand Floridian Resort and Spa

The Grand Floridian Villas opened in 2013 and continue the Victorian theming of the rest of Walt Disney World's flagship resort. As the smallest DVC resort at Disney World, the Grand Floridian was also the second monorail resort to receive a DVC addition. Like Bay Lake Tower, the villas building at the Grand Floridian has its own lobby and check-in, so guests do not need to visit the main lobby when they first arrive. A covered walkway links the villas building to the main building, similar to how the Beach Club Villas building is connected to the main resort.

The Villas at the Grand Floridian offer four different types of rooms. Deluxe studios are one of the largest at 374 square feet. The Grand Floridian was the first DVC resort that was built to accommodate up to five guests in a studio—other existing DVC resorts have been remodeled since then to do the same, and I expect any new DVC resorts or additions will also accommodate five guests in studio rooms. Deluxe studios have one queen bed, one full sleeper sofa, and one pull-down twin bunk. A kitchenette and a private porch or balcony are also included. Deluxe studios have some unique features, particularly in the bathroom, where the design was inspired by Disney Cruise Line ships; it is a split bathroom with one side having a shower and sink and the other side having a tub/shower and a toilet. Each side of the bathroom has a door into the room, as well as a door between the two bathroom halves. This allows two people to take a shower at the same time, almost like having two full baths. Disney incorporated this feature in response to guest feedback, showing they really do listen to their customers and try to improve upon what they already have. Another unique feature of the bathroom is a TV that is integrated into the mirror—maybe not a must-have feature, but still very cool. Deluxe studios are available as either a standard or lake view.

One-bedroom villas have 844 square feet and sleep five guests. They have one king bed, one queen sleeper sofa, and one pull-down twin bunk bed. The bathroom is a split design, similar to the deluxe studio, but this time there is a sink in each half, and the tub has a whirlpool. The room also has a washer and dryer, full kitchen, dining area, living area, and a private porch or balcony that extends across the entire width of the room, with entrances from both the bedroom and living area. The one-bedroom villa is also available as either a standard or lake view.

Two-bedroom villas are 1232 square feet, sleep up to nine guests, and are available as either a lockoff or dedicated villa, and as either a standard or lake view. Lockoff villas have one king bed, one queen bed, one queen sleeper sofa, one full sleeper sofa, and one pull-down twin bunk bed. Dedicated villas have one king bed, two queen beds, one queen sleeper sofa, and one pull-down bunk bed. These rooms have three full bathrooms, a washer and dryer, full kitchen, dining area, living area, and a private porch or balcony that spans the entire width of the room with entrances from both bedrooms and the living area.

Three-bedroom grand villas at the Grand Floridian are the largest currently available, at a whopping 2800 square feet! These rooms sleep up to twelve guests with one king bed, four queen beds, and a queen sleeper sofa. The grand villa is well-appointed: it has a grand entrance area, a media room with a home theater system, a huge living and dining area, four bathrooms, a washer and dryer, and two huge balconies—one off of the master suite and media room, the other off of the second and third bedrooms. The grand villa is also available as either a standard or lake view. While most grand villas at DVC resorts are two levels, the grand villa at the Grand Floridian is unique in that it is all on one level. You might think this room would cost you more vacation points than any other DVC room, but it is actually in second place—we'll talk about the most expensive room when we take a look at the Polynesian Village Resort in the next section.

The Grand Floridian is Walt Disney World's flagship resort. With its Victorian elegance echoing the architecture found on Main Street, USA, the Grand Floridian is a destination unto itself. Its many recreation options include two pools: the Courtyard Pool and the Beach Pool. The Courtyard Pool is a zero-entry pool located between the guest room buildings that features a hot tub, cabanas, and the Courtyard Pool Bar. The Beach Pool, as you might expect, is located next to the beach between the main resort and the villas building. The Beach Pool is also a zero-entry pool and features a slide, an Alice in Wonderland-themed water playground for kids, a hot tub, and the Beaches Pool Bar. Other recreation at the Grand Floridian includes the Captain's Shipyard marina where you can rent watercraft, the Senses Spa and Fitness Center, jogging trails, and an arcade. Within the main building's lobby you can enjoy live entertainment: piano and singer during the day, and a dedicated orchestra in the evening. At night, you can view the Magic Kingdom fireworks from a few different locations—either outside of the Gasparilla Grill restaurant or along the white sand beach that stretches between the Grand Floridian and Polynesian. You can also view nightly showings of the Electrical Water Pageant, a light show presented in front of each resort that is located on either Seven Seas Lagoon or Bay Lake.

There is a seemingly endless list of dining options at Disney's Grand Floridian, for all types of budgets. Besides the pool bars listed above, there's also Gasparilla Island Grill, 24-hour counter service restaurant. The Grand Floridian Café is an often overlooked table-service restaurant serving traditional American fare. Mizner's Lounge is a great place to enjoy some drinks or appetizers, and the Garden View Lounge is a small tea room that serves traditional afternoon tea along with character-themed parties. If you are looking for a great character dining option, try 1900 Park Fare, an "all-you-care-to-enjoy" buffet similar in price and atmosphere to Beach Club's Cape May Café. Narcoossee's and Citrico's are two upscale table-service restaurants at the Grand Floridian. Citrico's serves dinner nightly and features American food with a Mediterranean flair. Narcoossee's is a waterside restaurant with great views of the Seven Seas Lagoon as well as the Magic Kingdom fireworks and electrical water pageant if you time your reservation appropriately. Narcoossee's is also unique in that it features an open kitchen. For those with a more generous budget, or those just looking for a truly special dining experience, Victoria and Albert's is a AAA Five Diamond Award-winning table service restaurant with a different menu created nightly. Victoria and Albert's features three unique experiences, each having its own menu and wine selections: the main dining room, Queen Victoria's Room, and the Chef's Table. Be advised that Victoria and Albert's is very upscale and, as such, is an adults-only restaurant.

The Grand Floridian is one of three monorail resorts located at Walt Disney World, so getting to the Magic Kingdom, Epcot, or any of the other monorail resorts is quite easy. There's also boat and bus transportation. Located between the Grand Floridian and Polynesian resorts is Disney's Wedding Pavilion, headquarters of Disney's wedding planners. The Grand Floridian even features its own convention center.

For many people the Grand Floridian exemplifies the "ultimate" Disney resort. The points required to stay at the Grand Floridian are at the top end of all Walt Disney World DVC resorts. Even if you aren't staying here, it's a worthwhile stop to include on your itinerary. While staying at the Grand Floridian may fall outside of your budget, the Disney Vacation Club may afford you the option of staying at this wonderful resort!

Disney's Polynesian Villas & Bungalows

Disney's newest DVC resort is the Polynesian Villas & Bungalows. While the Polynesian was an original hotel when Walt Disney World opened in 1971, it was the last of the monorail resorts to receive a DVC addition. This addition opened in 2015 and includes three longhouses that were converted from standard hotel rooms to DVC deluxe studios, as well as twenty unique over-the-water bungalows built over Seven Seas Lagoon. These two-bedroom bungalows have a large outside deck with a private plunge pool and are currently the most expensive of all DVC accommodations. The Polynesian is unique in that it does not offer a one-bedroom option; however, it is possible to book connecting studio rooms. Let's take a look at the two room types available at Disney's Polynesian Villas & Bungalows.

The deluxe studio, at 460 square feet, is the largest DVC deluxe studio available. These rooms comfortably accommodate up to five guests with one queen bed, one queen sleeper sofa, and one pull-down twin bunk. The Polynesian studios have a split bathroom design similar to the deluxe studios at the Grand Floridian, though both halves of the bathroom here have a sink and there is no door that connects the halves. One bathroom has a tub/shower, toilet, and sink, and the other has a shower (with a rain feature) and sink. The room also features a kitchenette and private porch or balcony. You can choose from either standard view or lake view, depending on your vacation point budget.

The other type of room available at the Polynesian, and the most expensive DVC room in Walt Disney World, is the over-the-water two-bedroom bungalow. The bungalow is 1650 square feet and accommodates up to eight guests with one king bed, one queen bed, one queen sleeper sofa, and two pull-down twin bunk beds. The bungalow sits on stilts over Seven Seas Lagoon and has a large private deck with a plunge pool. You can watch the nightly Magic Kingdom fireworks from your deck, which also includes speakers that have the soundtrack for the nightly show. The bungalows have two bedrooms, two bathrooms, a full kitchen, and a huge dining and living area, as well as a washer and dryer.

The Polynesian Village Resort is extremely popular and has been ever since Walt Disney World opened in 1971. As one of the original resorts, a DVC presence at the Polynesian has been a wish of many DVC members for a long time. From the relaxing atmosphere of the resort to its great dining options, you can't go wrong at the Polynesian. You'll love its proximity to the Magic Kingdom—you can take a monorail directly there, or even opt for a relaxing boat ride. I love that the Polynesian, and in particular the DVC longhouses, sit right next to the Transportation and Ticket Center, which means you can easily walk over and get on the monorail to Epcot. The Polynesian has two pools—the main feature pool was recently redone and is themed around a volcano with water slides running through it. There is also a new kid's splash area and hot tub. The quiet pool, at press time, is also being redone and is scheduled to re-open sometime in 2016.

In terms of dining, there are several options at the Polynesian, and you're a short monorail ride away from the plethora of dining options at the Magic Kingdom, Contemporary, and Grand Floridian. The main quick-service dining location at the Polynesian is Captain Cook's, which has recently been refurbished and offers some unique menu items that will have you forgetting it's a counter-service meal. Aloha Isle offers one of my favorite Disney treats—the popular Dole Whip soft-served pineapple treat. 'Ohana is a very popular "all-you-care-to-enjoy" (Disney's way of saying "all-you-can-eat") table-service restaurant that features character dining. It's not a buffet; rather, the meal is served family-style with plates of food. 'Ohana is so popular that it can be difficult to obtain reservations, but if you are able to get one, it's well worth it. Kona Café is another table-service restaurant at the Polynesian, specializing in Tonga Toast for breakfast. Located next to Kona Café is Kona Island, a coffee bar in the morning and a sushi bar in the evening. The Tambu Lounge offers some great drinks and appetizers. Recently opened, Trader Sam's Grog Grotto and Tiki Terrace offer many amazing beverages, both alcoholic and non-alcoholic, as well as appetizers and snacks. Some of Trader Sam's drinks are even available with a souvenir mug. The Polynesian is also home to the Spirit of Aloha dinner show. Here you will enjoy an all-you-can-eat feast including BBQ ribs, chicken, pulled pork, and other Polynesian-inspired dishes, all while enjoying a high-energy show featuring hula dancers, drummers, and fire-knife performers.

The Polynesian's location is one of my favorite features of this resort. You can easily view the Magic Kingdom fireworks from the beach here, and they even pump in the music so that you feel like you are right inside the park without having to deal with the crowds. Disney also features nightly showings of the Electrical Water Pageant, a light show presented in front of each resort that is located on Seven Seas Lagoon or Bay Lake.

I encourage you to visit the Polynesian, even if you aren't staying there. It is another resort where the theming takes over and makes you feel like you've been transported to a Hawaiian paradise. It's a great resort to visit at night for a few different reasons, including the large flaming torches along the walking paths and the sandy beach where you can find a hammock or chair from which to watch the fireworks.

Due to its premium location and status as one of Walt Disney's World's most sought-after resorts, the points required to stay at the Polynesian are among the highest and on par with the Grand Floridian. Prior to joining DVC, I would have never been able to afford a cash reservation here, but now that I'm a DVC member, I can. The only hard part may be getting a reservation here.

In addition to all of the resorts we just talked about, Disney has four additional vacation club properties outside of Walt Disney World. Let's take a look at what each of these resorts has to offer.

Disney's Vero Beach Resort

Disney's Vero Beach Resort was the first DVC resort to open outside of Walt Disney World, in 1995. This resort, located along the Atlantic Coast, offers a taste of Old Florida. There are five different types of rooms available.

The deluxe inn room is 360 square feet and sleeps up to four guests with two queen beds. The room also features one bathroom, a kitchenette, private porch or balcony, and either a garden or ocean view.

The studio villa is 370 square feet and accommodates four guests with a queen bed and full sleeper sofa. The room includes one bathroom, a kitchenette, and a private porch or balcony.

One-bedroom villas are 880 square feet and sleep up to four guests, plus one guest under three years of age. These rooms have one king bed, one queen sleeper sofa, one bathroom, a washer and dryer, full kitchen, dining area, living area, and private porch or balcony.

Two-bedroom villas are 1255 square feet and can sleep eight guests, plus one guest under three. These rooms have one king bed, one queen bed, one queen sleeper sofa, and one full sleeper sofa. Two-bedroom villas have two bathrooms, a washer and dryer, full kitchen, dining area, living area, and private porch or balcony.

The largest room type available at Disney's Vero Beach Resort is the three-bedroom beach cottage at 2125 square feet. The room sleeps twelve guests, plus one guest under three. Beach cottages have one king bed, four queen beds, and one queen sofa sleeper. The three bathrooms in this cottage will assure that everyone has the space and privacy they need. A full kitchen, dining area, and living area complete the room. A private porch is located on the lower level while a private balcony awaits on the second level.

There are four dining locations at Disney's Vero Beach DVC resort. Shutters is a casual table-service restaurant featuring seafood and weekend character brunches. Sonya's is a formal table-service restaurant featuring steaks, chops, and seafood. The Green Cabin Room is a full-service bar located above the lobby, with additional seating on a deck that overlooks the Atlantic Ocean. Bleacher's is a poolside quick-service food and drink counter.

Vero Beach offers plenty of recreational opportunities as well. The resort features a pool shaped like Mickey Mouse with a slide. The pool is surrounded by a Peter Pan-themed 9-hole miniature golf course. The community hall features activities like table tennis, pool, and arts and crafts. There's also an arcade, fitness center, volleyball courts, soccer fields, tennis courts, and basketball hoop.

Many folks overlook this resort because it is not near one of the Disney theme parks, but it can be a great add-on to a Disney cruise, a Walt Disney World trip, or even just a trip on its own.

Disney's Hilton Head Island Resort

Located on a secluded 15-acre island in the Shelter Cove Harbour area, Disney's Hilton Head Island Resort opened in 1996. This resort has a rustic "South Carolina Lowcountry" theme. A shuttle bus transports guests from the resort to Disney's Beach House in Palmetto Dunes, a little over a mile away from the resort, where guests can enjoy the beach as well as a pool area.

There are four different types of rooms at Disney's Hilton Head Island Resort, starting with the studio villa at 455 square feet. Sleeping up to four guests, the studio villa includes one queen bed, one full sleeper sofa, one bathroom, a kitchenette, and a private porch or balcony.

Next up is the one-bedroom villa at 856 square feet. Sleeping four guests, plus one guest under three years of age, this room includes one king bed, one queen sleeper sofa, one bathroom, a washer and dryer, full kitchen, dining area, and living area. A private balcony is also included and has entrances off of both the living area and bedroom.

Two-bedroom villas at Hilton Head are 1245 square feet and sleep up to eight guests, plus one guest under three. These villas have one king bed, two queen beds, and one queen sleeper sofa. The room includes two bathrooms, a washer and dryer, full kitchen, dining area, living area, and private balcony with entrances off of both the main bedroom and living area.

Finally, the three-bedroom grand villa is the largest room type available at Hilton Head. The grand villa has 2363 square feet and sleeps up to twelve guests, plus one guest under three. The room spans two levels and includes one king bed, four queen beds, one queen sofa sleeper, three bathrooms, a washer and dryer, full kitchen, dining area, and living area. A private porch is located on the lower level.

Dining options at Disney's Hilton Head Island Resort are somewhat limited compared to the other DVC resorts. There is no table-service restaurant located at the resort itself; however, there are many restaurants located in close proximity to the resort, and some are even within walking distance. The resort does offer counter-service dining at both the main resort pool (Tide Me Over), and at the beach house (Signals). There is also a full-service bar, Surfman's Sand Bar, located at the beach house.

Disney's Hilton Head Island has many activities for children, including campfires, arts and crafts, swimming and pool games, magic shows, and even crabbing. Adults can enjoy many of the same activities, plus kayaking, biking, and tennis.

Disney's Hilton Head Island Resort is a great resort to visit if you want to try something different than the typical Disney vacation. A stay here may even be a bit more relaxing because you are not in the middle of the hustle and bustle of the theme parks. The great thing about the Disney Vacation Club is that there is quite a bit of variety in the resorts, and there's nothing wrong with trying new things.

The Villas at Disney's Grand Californian Resort & Spa

The Grand Californian Resort is the only DVC resort located at the Disneyland Resort in Anaheim, California. The resort was opened in 2001 and underwent an expansion in 2009 to add additional rooms and Disney Vacation Club villas.

There are four different types of rooms at Disney's Grand Californian, starting with the studio villa at 379 square feet. This room accommodates up to four guests and features one queen bed, one queen sleeper sofa, one bathroom, a kitchenette, and a private porch or balcony.

One-bedroom villas are the next size up at 865 square feet. One bedrooms sleep up to five guests with one king bed, one queen sleeper sofa, and one pull-out bunk bed. The room has two bathrooms, a washer and dryer, full kitchen, dining area, and living area. A private porch or balcony is located off of the bedroom.

Two-bedroom villas are 1257 square feet, sleep up to nine guests, and are available as either a lockoff configuration or dedicated. Lockoff villas have one king bed, one queen bed, two queen sleeper sofas, and one pull-out bunk bed. Dedicated villas have one king bed, two queen beds, one queen sleeper sofa, and one pull-out bunk bed. Other features of the room include three bathrooms, a washer and dryer, full kitchen, dining area, and living area. There are two private balconies, one off of each bedroom.

The three-bedroom grand villa, at 2426 square feet, is the largest room available at Disney's Grand Californian Resort. It sleeps twelve guests and features one king bed, four queen beds, one queen sofa sleeper, and one full sofa sleeper. Other features of the grand villa include four bathrooms, a washer and dryer, full kitchen, huge dining area, and a huge living area. Like most DVC grand villas, it spans two levels, with the master suite, kitchen, living room, and dining room on the first level, and two additional bedrooms and a living area on the second level. The room has a private balcony off of each bedroom as well as the dining room.

The flagship restaurant here is Napa Rose, a table-service restaurant featuring large windows overlooking Disney's California Adventure theme park. The Storyteller's Café serves grilled items and home-style dishes. White Water Snacks is a quick service snack bar.

The Grand Californian is the sister resort to the Grand Floridian at Walt Disney World, though the theming between the two is different. While the Grand Floridian has a Victorian theme reminiscent of Main Street, USA, the Grand Californian is a luxury resort designed after the 20th century arts-and-crafts era that was prominent in northern California. The Grand Californian is unique in that is has an entrance directly into Disney's California Adventure theme park, located in the Grizzly Peak area.

The Grand Californian resort is not to be missed if you are visiting Disneyland. As the only DVC resort in or around Disneyland, rooms here can be difficult to come by. I have never stayed here, but it is definitely on my DVC bucket list!

Aulani Disney Vacation Club Villas

Located on the Hawaiian island of Oahu, Disney's much-anticipated Aulani Resort & Spa opened in 2011 with 259 hotel rooms and 460 DVC villas. The resort sits on 21 acres of prime, oceanfront property and is themed to celebrate the customs and traditions of the Hawaiian people.

There are five different types of rooms available to DVC members at Disney's Aulani Resort, starting with the hotel room at 382 square feet. It can accommodate up to four guests with either two queen beds or one king bed and one queen sleeper sofa. The room also has one bathroom and a private balcony. This room differs from most other DVC resort rooms in that it does not have a kitchenette. Only standard view rooms are available for this category.

Next up is the studio villa at 356 square feet. It can accommodate up to four guests with a queen bed and queen sleeper sofa. The room also has one bathroom, a kitchenette, and a private balcony. There are four view types available: standard, island gardens, poolside gardens, or ocean.

One-bedroom villas are 755 square feet and sleep up to five guests with one king bed, one queen sleeper sofa, and one pull-down bunk bed. Other features include one bathroom, a washer and dryer, full kitchen, dining area, and living area. There are two private balconies, one off of the bedroom and one off of the living area. Standard, island gardens, poolside gardens, or ocean view studios are available.

Two-bedroom villas are 1125 square feet and sleep up to nine guests. These rooms are available as either a lockoff or dedicated configuration. Lockoff villas have one king bed, one queen bed, two queen sleeper sofas, and one pull-down bunk bed, while dedicated villas have one king bed, two queen beds, one queen sleeper sofa, and one twin sleeper chair. This villa has two-and-a-half bathrooms, a washer and dryer, full kitchen, dining area, and living area. Dedicated villas have two balconies—one off of the main bedroom and another with entrances from both the second bedroom and the living area. Lockoff villas have three balconies—one off of each bedroom and one off of the living area. Standard, island gardens, poolside gardens, or ocean views are available.

Three-bedroom grand villas are 2174 square feet and sleep up to twelve guests. They feature one king bed, four queen beds, and two queen sofa sleepers. Grand villas have three bathrooms, a full kitchen, dining room, living room, washer and dryer, and a huge balcony with entrances from each bedroom as well as both the living room and dining room. Like the Grand Floridian grand villas, the ones here also occupy one level. Only standard or ocean view rooms are available in this category.

Aulani features an elaborate pool and play area as well as an 18,000 square foot spa. The pool area was expanded in 2013 and now includes a themed family infinity pool, giving the illusion that the pool spills into the ocean. The pool area has a kid's splash area and Keiki Cove, which resembles a tidal pool complete with pool creatures on the floor, water jets, and Menehune (these are the legendary little people of the Hawaiian Islands). The Wailana Pool is now an adults-only pool area; it was formerly the resort's quiet pool. There's also a children's club called Aunty's Beach House, two table-service restaurants, and six quick-service dining locations. 'Ama 'Ama and Makahiki are Aulani's table service restaurants. 'Ama 'Ama offers breakfast, lunch, and dinner, while Makahiki offers a breakfast buffet (with Disney characters three days out of the week), as well as an a-la-carte lunch and dinner. Prices for meals and refillable mugs at Aulani are typically higher than what you would find at Walt Disney World. In fact, most everything in Hawaii is fairly expensive, so it's important to plan your vacation budget accordingly.

Aulani is a fabulous resort. It is distinctively Disney, while still being distinctively Hawaiian, as well. If you're a Disney fan and have always dreamed of visiting Hawaii, I encourage you to check out Aulani.

Now that we've taken a look at each of the DVC resorts, let's talk about what the future looks like for DVC. You might be wondering if new DVC resorts are going to be added, or you might ask whether the DVC program will be the same 40–50 years from now as your contract gets closer to expiration. I can tell you with great confidence that the future of DVC is bright and there will be more DVC resorts opening in the coming years. In fact, I believe that most resort construction at Walt Disney World in the near future will likely be DVC additions instead of traditional hotels. DVC rooms already account for about 10% of the rooms at Walt Disney World, and even at that level Disney has been hard-pressed to keep up with demand. Right now it's difficult to book a DVC reservation less than seven months out unless you are going to one of the larger resorts like Saratoga Springs.

The DVC program is mutually beneficial to both the Walt Disney Company and DVC members. As DVC increases, Disney can rely on more and more repeat visitors. While these visitors have already paid for their hotel stays up front when they bought their contract, they still have to buy tickets, food, and merchandise. And DVC members benefit by locking in hotel costs at today's prices for the remainder of their DVC contract. Disney has always called DVC their best-kept secret, but every day more and more people are finding out about it and buying in.

Disney has recently announced plans to expand the DVC presence at Wilderness Lodge. While details are not fully known, Disney announced it will build lakeside cabins along the shores of Bay Lake— similar to the Bora Bora Over-the-Water bungalows at the Polynesian Village. Beyond the Wilderness Lodge project, there have also been rumors in recent years that Disney may look into adding a DVC presence at one of the moderate resorts, particularly the Caribbean Beach.

A few years ago Disney had plans to build a stand-alone DVC resort between the Fort Wilderness Resort & Campground and Wilderness Lodge (where the remains of the closed River Country water park still stand). This resort was to be known as "Buffalo Junction". Rumor has it that Disney was actually only days away from breaking ground when it decided to hold off on the Buffalo Junction project and add a DVC presence at the Polynesian Village instead. The thinking was that they wanted to have a DVC presence at each of the monorail hotels first. While those plans were shelved, I do believe that the Buffalo Junction DVC resort will eventually see the light of day. Maybe it's just wishful thinking on my part, but I would love to see the River Country property used again.

Disney also recently announced plans to add a Star Wars land and Toy Story land to Hollywood Studios. This announcement, coupled with the recent addition of New Fantasyland at the Magic Kingdom and the construction of Pandora at the Animal Kingdom, will only draw more and more folks to Walt Disney World in the coming years.

It's possible that Disney may add new DVC resorts outside of Disney World, but for now I think the focus continues to be increasing the number of DVC rooms there. The Walt Disney Company as a whole is very strong financially, and they are undergoing a period of remarkable growth, so DVC is bound to grow along with it. The future of DVC is very bright!

NINE

Frequently Asked Questions

Sometimes it can be more helpful to learn about the ins and outs of the Disney Vacation Club by looking at common questions that typically arise when discussing DVC. The questions below are from potential members as well as new members who are trying to use their membership and points in the most efficient manner. Consider this chapter to be a quick-reference guide to DVC.

Which Disney Vacation Club resorts are available for purchase?

As Disney opens new resorts, real estate shares become available for purchase. As of 2015, Disney has two resorts that are available for purchase: Disney's Polynesian Villas & Bungalows and Disney's Aulani resort in Hawaii. While DVC contracts at these two resorts are available for direct-purchase from Disney, you have the ability to purchase a contract at any DVC resort via the resale market. If you inquire with Disney you may be able to do a direct-purchase into the other vacation club resorts, but prices will not be much lower than the new resorts that are being offered, and the contract term will be shorter. So, if you are looking for a DVC contract at a resort other than what is being offered for direct purchase, you are usually much better off buying a DVC contract on the resale market.

What accommodations can I expect at a DVC resort?

DVC rooms are designed to make you feel like you are at home. One-bedroom, two-bedroom, and three-bedroom villas include master suites, full kitchens, dining and living areas, and a washer and dryer.

Deluxe studios require the least amount of points to book and are similar to a standard hotel room except that the deluxe studio will have a kitchenette in most cases. Most deluxe studios accommodate up to four people, and some studios have a pull-down bunk to accommodate a fifth guest. One bedrooms typically hold 4–5 people, two bedrooms hold 8–9, and three bedrooms up to 12 people.

If I join DVC, will I be guaranteed a room at Walt Disney World?

You may be surprised to find that the answer is no. While DVC is a timeshare, it works differently from traditional "fixed-week" timeshares. DVC is operated on a points system, so while you are guaranteed to receive points each year to use toward your Disney vacation, room reservations are subject to availability. It will typically be easier for you to obtain reservations at your home resort because you can make reservations up to 11 months prior to your check-in, while non-home resorts have a 7-month booking window. There are certain times of the year for which it will be difficult to obtain a reservation, such as during the summer months as well as spring break and most holidays. In general, as long as you can make your trip plans 7 months or more in advance, you should be able to find accommodations at one of the Disney Vacation Club resorts. If you can't find a reservation for all nights at one resort, consider booking a split stay at two different DVC resorts. Disney will move your bags between resorts at no charge. This is also a great way to experience a new resort that you may have never tried before.

Can I stay at a Disney Vacation Club resort if I am not a DVC member?

Surprisingly, yes—you can stay at a DVC resort even if you are not a DVC member. There are a few different ways to do so. First, you can make a cash reservation with Disney. Disney holds some rooms at DVC resorts for cash reservations; however, these are typically very expensive, with the price on par with, or often even more than, the cost of a deluxe resort. While expensive, this can actually be a good way to try out DVC and see how you like the resorts and rooms before purchasing a contract. Another way to stay at a DVC resort without being a member is by renting points from an existing DVC member. You can then use those points to book a trip. Lastly, if you own a timeshare that has an exchange program with DVC, you can exchange your timeshare for a DVC stay (similar to the way DVC members can exchange their points for stays at other timeshare resorts).

What is the member getaways program?

This program allows DVC members to experience much more than just Disney resorts—there are literally thousands of destinations around the world for which you can exchange your DVC points. Note that if you have a resale contract, there are limits on which non-Disney resorts you can book.

Is DVC better than buying or renting a vacation home?

Simply put, flexibility of the DVC program and the Disney magic! While some vacation homes may require a full week's rental, DVC allows you to book for whatever length of stay works for you—whether it's 1 day, 4 days, 1 week, or even 1 month. Plus, if you buy a vacation home you are locked in to staying in that one location, where with the DVC you have many options. The great thing about staying at a DVC resort is that you know it will be impeccably maintained by Disney, and you don't need a rental car or taxi to get around—you can use Disney's Magical Express at no charge to get you from the airport to your resort, and then use Disney transportation to get you anywhere on Disney property, all free of charge.

What is a use year?

The use year is the month in which you receive your yearly allotment of points. If your use year is September, you will receive your points on September 1 and they will expire August 31 of the following year, unless you decide to bank the points (keep in mind that you must bank points within the first 8 months of your use year).

Once I buy into DVC, are my vacations totally paid off for the lifetime of my contract?

I wish that were true, but there are yearly costs to consider. You will have to pay yearly maintenance fees, typically ranging from about $4.90 to $7.75 per point, depending on which DVC resort is your home resort. These yearly maintenance fees can be paid in a lump sum in January of each year, or they can be spread across 12 monthly payments for no extra fees or interest. Also remember that your DVC membership takes care of the hotel accommodations only; you will still need to pay for food, tickets, and merchandise, though as a DVC member you'll enjoy discounts on all of these things. Make sure you pay your maintenance fees on time each year, as failure to do so may put your DVC contract into foreclosure and void any reservations you have already made.

What is the banking deadline?

When banking points, you must do so by eight months following your current use year. For example, if your use year is September, you have until May of the following year to bank your points. If they are not banked, you must "use them or lose them". Disney may make a one-time exception to this rule if it was truly an oversight, but I caution you not to rely on this—bank your points on time!

What is a waitlisted reservation?

When booking reservations, if the date(s) that you need are not available at a particular resort or for a specific room style, you can create a waitlist in case someone cancels. Waitlists are filled based on the order in which they were created. You can have up to two waitlists at one time. A waitlist can be for a single day or a block of multiple days, but if you make a waitlist for a block of multiple days, all of those days would have to open up at the same time for the waitlist to be fulfilled. It's usually a better strategy to waitlist one day at a time.

What if I'm just a few points short for booking a trip and don't want to borrow any points from the next use year, or don't have any available to borrow?

Never fear, the DVC program is flexible. You can buy a limited number of extra points directly from Disney. These points are called "one-time use" points. They are not added to your contract, meaning you will not receive these points each year, just the one time that you need them to complete a particular reservation. You can purchase up to 24 of these extra points per year, but there are restrictions on how they can be used. They are non-transferrable, non-refundable, and can't be banked or borrowed. They can only be used in the 7-month booking window, they are not available for waitlisted reservations, and they cannot be applied retroactively to existing reservations. Your account must also be in good standing (up-to-date on maintenance fees).

How long does it take to close on a resale contract?

Generally, it will take about 8 weeks from the time you submit an offer to the time you have all of your membership documents and can make a DVC reservation. The main variable that will affect how quickly your contract closes is how fast you and the seller respond to each other on offers, and how quickly you and the seller sign your paperwork. Disney's right-of-first refusal (ROFR) process draws the timeframe out, but Disney almost always take the entire 30 days (or very close to it) to complete this process, so there's not much you can do to change that aspect of buying resale.

When will I receive my DVC welcome packet (member ID card, new member handbook, vacation planner)?

Approximately 45 days after closing. You can call member services earlier to see if you are able to get your member ID over the phone if you need to make a reservation before you get your welcome packet.

What if I no longer want my DVC contract?

If you buy a DVC contract and find that it doesn't work for you, or if you need to get rid of it for financial reasons, you do have options. A DVC membership is a real estate interest, so you can sell it just as you would sell your house. I recommend selling your contract through a reputable broker that specializes in timeshare sales and, in particular, DVC resales. Additionally, you can will your DVC membership to somebody in the event that you pass away. This is a great perk for older vacationers who know that their DVC contract will outlive them, but want to leave a lasting vacation for their children and grandchildren.

Do all nights cost the same amount of points?

No, the amount of points required to book a room at a DVC resort varies widely based on what type of room you want (deluxe dtudio, one bedroom, two bedroom, three bedroom, etc.), the time of year (for example, summer costs more points than less busy times of the year such as September), the night of the week (Fridays and Saturdays cost more than the other days of the week), and the DVC resort you choose to stay at. Each DVC resort has a chart that details how many points are required to book each room type during each season. These points do not change year-over-year, so when you buy into DVC you are essentially locking in today's rates for future vacations.

Is there a limit to how many vacation points I can buy?

There is a limit, although only the wealthiest need concern themselves about it. Earlier in this book I wrote that the typical DVC contract is about 150 points. The maximum point rule is 2,000 points at a single resort, but you can have multiple DVC contracts at different resorts, with the total for all combined contracts set at 5,000 points. Now, there are ways to get around this rule. For example, you can put some contracts in your name and some in your spouse's name. Or you could set up trusts to get even more. In reality, most of us will never need to worry about the maximum number of points—imagine how much your yearly maintenance fees would be on 5000 points!

TEN

Before You Go

You should now have a pretty good idea of whether DVC is right for you, and you should have the knowledge you need to take the next step. That next step is scary, but you will be glad you took it.

Once you have bought a DVC contract, I must warn you of what's to come.

There is a rare condition that many DVC members suffer from; in fact, the condition is usually worst amongst first-time DVC members: "add-on-itis". You may think the only cure for this condition is buying more DVC points; however, in some cases that just feeds the condition and makes you want even more points. It's inevitable, once you become a DVC member, you are going to want to get more points. I'm not sure that I've ever met a DVC member who doesn't crave more points—it seems to be an insatiable desire that takes a lot of willpower to overcome.

Once you start using your DVC contract, it will change the way you vacation at Walt Disney World forever. It will cause you to want to visit for longer periods of time or visit multiple times per year, or even both. You may even find that you want to upgrade from staying in a deluxe studio room to staying in a one-bedroom villa, or an even larger room. Some folks may even want to use their DVC membership to vacation with extended family in a grand villa. There will be so many reasons floating through your head as to why you should buy more points. I don't know if you can ever have enough DVC points!

But I advise that you be very careful when adding DVC points. First, make sure you consider the financial ramifications of adding on. Don't mortgage your future if you can't really afford it. Remember that you will need to pay maintenance fees on the points you have now as well as the points you add on. One of the biggest reasons that people end up with foreclosures on their DVC contracts is unpaid maintenance fees. If you're late on those fees, Disney may freeze your account so that you are unable to make reservations. If you're account goes into foreclosure, you're going to have to pay not only the unpaid maintenance fees, but also interest and legal fees. It can fast become a slippery slope. So, whatever you do, make sure your budget allows for extra points. Also, don't forget that you'll still need to pay for food, park passes, and souvenirs for each visit—and these can be substantial, especially if you plan to visit a DVC resort more than once a year.

With that said, we've now come to the end of this book. While my primary objective was to give you the tools you need to evaluate, buy, and use the Disney Vacation Club, I also hope that you were entertained along the way, and now have a clear direction of what you want to do next. If you are already a DVC member, I hope the tips that I've offered have given you new insight into the program.

Never let anyone pressure you into purchasing a DVC contract. While DVC may make sense for many, it is not for everyone. Make sure you look not only at how you currently vacation, but also how you want to vacation in the future. Figuring out that the Disney Vacation Club isn't right for you is better discovered up front, before you actually go out and buy a DVC contract that you will soon regret.

If you do think DVC is right for you, I encourage you to join as soon as possible. Prices are only going to continue to go up and the earlier you can join the better. Most of the time people are not disappointed that they joined DVC, only that they didn't do it sooner, and I am certainly in that category. Looking at historical prices for both direct and resale purchases, I wish I had joined sooner, but at the same time I'm also happy that my wife and I waited until we had fully researched DVC before jumping in with both feet. The extra time we took to make our decision was a good thing—we were able to discover resale as a viable buy-in avenue for our family. Buying a resale contract turned out to be a great fit for us. We were able to find a contract that fit us perfectly in terms of contract size, home resort, and use year. If you pursue a resale contract, remember that you're going to need patience during the process.

I've been a huge fan of Walt Disney World since my first trip there with my parents over 30 years ago. It has changed immensely since that time, adding two theme parks, two waterparks, and numerous resorts and restaurants. Knowing that I'll be able to continue to watch it grow over the coming decades while sharing the Disney magic with my wife and kids gives me great joy and satisfaction. Becoming members of the Disney Vacation Club has helped us realize that dream of vacationing with Disney each and every year, and it can do the same for you.

Thank you so much for reading this book. I look forward to hearing how it helps you realize your Disney dreams.

About the Author

Shaun Brouwer has over 20 years of experience planning Walt Disney World vacations and operates a website to help others plan their own Walt Disney World vacations: PlanWDW.com. He is interested in all things Disney, particularly Walt Disney World history and the man that started it all, Walt Disney. Shaun has been visiting Walt Disney World for over 30 years and loves making Disney memories with his wife, Jamie, and their three kids, Zach, Kyle, and Ashleigh.

More Books from Theme Park Press

Theme Park Press publishes dozens of books each year for Disney fans and for general and academic audiences. Here are just a few of our titles. For the complete catalog, including book descriptions and excerpts, please visit:

ThemeParkPress.com

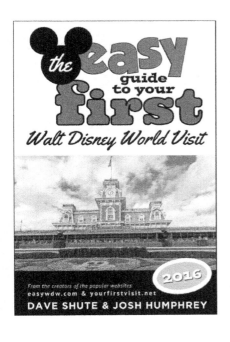

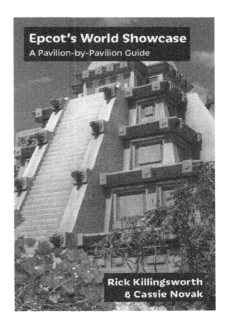

DISNEY
BY THE
NUMBERS

FACTS AND FIGURES ABOUT THE WALT DISNEY WORLD THEME PARKS AND RESORTS

ANTHONY M. CASELNOVA

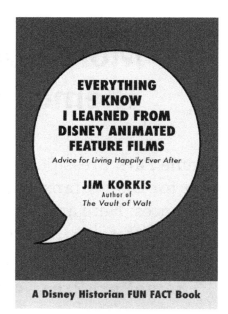

EVERYTHING I KNOW I LEARNED FROM DISNEY ANIMATED FEATURE FILMS

Advice for Living Happily Ever After

JIM KORKIS
Author of
The Vault of Walt

A Disney Historian FUN FACT Book

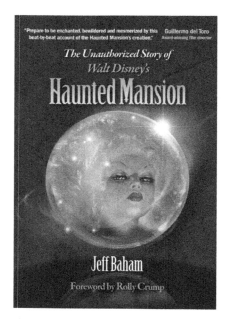

"Prepare to be enchanted, bewildered and mesmerized by this beat-by-beat account of the Haunted Mansion's creation." — Guillermo del Toro, Award-winning film director

The Unauthorized Story of
Walt Disney's
Haunted Mansion

Jeff Baham

Foreword by Rolly Crump

A Historical Tour of
Walt Disney World

Jungle Cruise · Pirates of the Caribbean · Enchanted Tiki Room · Crystal Palace · Main Street, U.S.A. · Carousel of Progress · Tomorrowland

VOLUME I

ANDREW KISTE

501
WAYS TO MAKE THE MOST OF
YOUR WALT DISNEY WORLD
VACATION

Kristi Fredericks

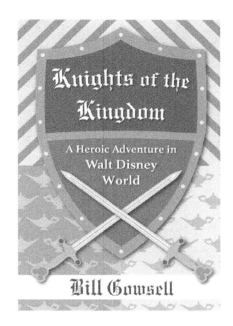

Knights of the
Kingdom

A Heroic Adventure in
Walt Disney
World

Bill Gowsell

Walt Disney
AND THE PROMISE OF
Progress City

SAM GENNAWEY
Foreword by Werner Weiss

THE
RIDE DELEGATE
Memoir of a Walt Disney World VIP Tour Guide

Annie Salisbury

Sara

EARNS HER EARS

My Secret Walt Disney World
Cast Member Diary

SARA LOPES
Earning Your Ears: Volume Three

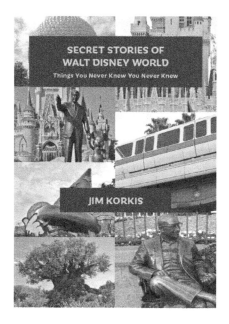

SECRET STORIES OF
WALT DISNEY WORLD
Things You Never Knew You Never Knew

JIM KORKIS

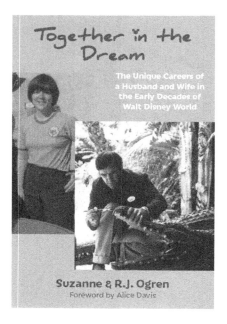

Together in the
Dream

The Unique Careers of
a Husband and Wife in
the Early Decades of
Walt Disney World

Suzanne & R.J. Ogren
Foreword by Alice Davis

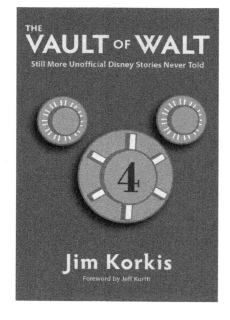

THE
VAULT OF WALT

Still More Unofficial Disney Stories Never Told

4

Jim Korkis
Foreword by Jeff Kurtti

Made in the USA
Monee, IL
06 May 2020